One Lamb
Redeemed

Donna & Family
Thank you for the blessing of
your ~~friendship~~ !
Shalom,
Shoshana

One Lamb Redeemed

Shoshana Goldberg

A True Life Story About an Ordinary Life Called
and Destined by an Extraordinary God

TATE PUBLISHING
AND ENTERPRISES, LLC

One Lamb Redeemed
Copyright © 2013 by Soshana Goldberg. All rights reserved.

Scripture quotations marked (CJB) are taken from the *Complete Jewish Bible*, copyright © 1998 by David H. Stern. Published by Jewish New Testament Publications, Inc. www.messianicjewish.net/jntp. Distributed by Messianic Jewish Resources. www.messianicjewish.net. All rights reserved. Used by permission.

Scripture quotations marked (NASB) are taken from the *New American Standard Bible®*, Copyright © 1960, 1962, 1963, 1968, 1971, 1972, 1973, 1975, 1977, 1995 by The Lockman Foundation. Used by permission.

This book is based on real events and people. In some instances, names, descriptions, and incidents included in the story have been changed.

This book is designed to provide accurate and authoritative information with regard to the subject matter covered. This information is given with the understanding that neither the author nor Tate Publishing, LLC is engaged in rendering legal, professional advice. Since the details of your situation are fact dependent, you should additionally seek the services of a competent professional.

The opinions expressed by the author are not necessarily those of Tate Publishing, LLC.

Published by Tate Publishing & Enterprises, LLC
127 E. Trade Center Terrace | Mustang, Oklahoma 73064 USA
1.888.361.9473 | www.tatepublishing.com

Tate Publishing is committed to excellence in the publishing industry. The company reflects the philosophy established by the founders, based on Psalm 68:11,
"The Lord gave the word and great was the company of those who published it."

Book design copyright © 2013 by Tate Publishing, LLC. All rights reserved.
Cover design by Allen Jomoc
Interior design by Mary Jean Archival

Published in the United States of America

ISBN: 978-1-62510-610-0
1. Biography & Autobiography / General
2. Biography & Autobiography / Religious
13.06.06

Dedication

This story is dedicated to Yeshua, our Messiah, the audience of One; the One who walked me through it all! It is also dedicated to my loving husband for standing with me through thick and thin. He is my hero!

I want to extend my heartfelt thanks to Regina Shank and the intercessors of Missouri Prayer. They are the best of the best!

Contents

Introduction

And they overcame him because of the blood
of the Lamb and because of the word of their
testimony and they did not love their life even
when faced with death.

Revelation 12:11 (NASB)

There have been a lot of sermons preached about
this scripture. Men have expounded on being
covered by the blood of Jesus and the importance of
our testimony; however, I don't recall much preaching
on not loving our lives even when facing death. After
all, we live in a relatively free society. Christians are not
routinely martyred for their faith in our land, so "part
C" of Revelation 12:11 isn't generally mentioned.

Death, however, can take many forms. If we lived
in the Middle East, North Africa, China, or any other
innumerable anti-Judeo-Christian nations we might be
faced with jail, torture, or physical death for the "word
of our testimony" about our Lord and Messiah Jesus.
We would be very careful when and with whom we
shared this vital information. If word got out that Jesus
was Lord, we'd be arrested and told in no uncertain

terms to renounce our faith in Him. Many of our lives would hang in the balance; some would be short-lived.

No, we are not afraid of these things, but there is such a thing as the death of our reputation, the loss of close relationship with our friends and family. I'm convinced it is just as painful. Most of us have been around long enough to see firsthand what misunderstanding, gossip, slander, and backbiting in the church can produce. Everywhere you go, there are walking wounded. Men and women, young and old, who refuse to step across the threshold of a church building ever again except for weddings and funerals. Some of these were believers who, when convicted by the Holy Spirit of their sin, were unwilling to repent and chose to walk away. I've met some of these. They know Jesus loves them and that they're sinners, but some have never had anyone patiently walk them through deliverance so they could be set free. They believe they are trapped for the rest of their lives. They have had Christians point the finger at them and gossip about them. These are trapped by fear, guilt, and condemnation. However, "Love covers a multitude of sins" (1 Peter 4:8b, NASB).

There are also many believers who faithfully serve the Lord and obey His Word. These are sensitive to the leading of His Spirit and allow His correction in their lives. They are also among the walking wounded. Maybe they didn't fit the traditional church mold. God said they could pray in an unknown language, but when they did, they were given the left foot of fellowship. Maybe they operated in the prophetic, brought forth a word of knowledge that someone didn't want to hear or had the boldness to witness for Jesus causing jealousy in the church leadership because they lacked that kind of boldness. Whatever it was, someone in the core group of the church got offended and shot the sheep. I've met a lot of these over the years; people with the call of God on their lives who love God with everything in them but don't contribute to a local church body. They are wounded and bleeding.

Because of all these things, the body of Christ is crippled. It is missing crucial parts and pieces that we have to have to win the lost and build His kingdom in these last days. It is for you, the walking wounded, that this book is written.

This is simply the story of my life. It is not a theological dissertation. Many men and women, much more learned than myself, have written a multitude of wonderful books that can teach you scripturally how to live for and walk with God (I have included a list of my favorites in appendix A). This is just a story about how the all-powerful God of the universe picked one very average person to do extraordinary things through. It can be the story of anyone's life. All a person has to do is simply put aside their insecurities and fears and trust and believe that Jesus can and wants to do amazing things through them.

I am, generally speaking, a private person, so the telling of my story is both difficult and at times painful; but the Lord asked that I do this. I am not allowed to pick and choose which part of Revelation 12:11 to obey, so in these pages, I open up my life to you, the reader, so that you might learn both from my victories and my failures. I choose not to love my life (reputation) even to the death. I have, however, chosen to use a "pen" name and also not to use anyone else's name in this book. I've done so to protect both the innocent and the guilty. (The guilty might repent!) I also don't wish to invade anyone's privacy or hurt anyone's feelings. This story is about what Jesus did in me and through me, not about other's responses to these events. Here is the story of a life lived in Jesus, the lover of my soul, the audience of One.

Beginnings

B'resheet is an interesting word. It is, basically, the Hebrew word for the beginning, but it is so much more. We are much more familiar with the Greek word *Genesis*. It is used in all English translations of our Bibles. The word *B'resheet* comes from the Hebrew letter Bet, meaning house and Resheet meaning first in place, time, order, or rank (specifically a firstfruit)[1]. In *A Year Through the Torah*, the author states that the numeric value for Bet is the same as the value for life. He says, "The house of creation is then the life of the universe." It also denotes "in": "suggesting God's intention of abiding within the realm of creation."[2]

God is all about relationship—Immanuel, God with us, living inside of us. The Holy Spirit wants to dwell in us (1 Corinthians 6:19). We are His temple. From the very beginning, God wanted to commune with mankind, fellowship with us—His creation. In Genesis 3:8, the Bible tells us that God walked in the garden with Adam and Eve "in the cool of the day," but the Hebrew word used there is *Ruach*. It means wind, breath, or spirit and is the same word used for the Holy Spirit. I doubt that Eden was too hot earlier in the day for the Lord to commune with them. I imagine that Eden was perfectly climate controlled. I also like to think that God wanted to fellowship with them more often than once a day. I think they walked in the very breath of His presence when they lived in Eden.

Many people look at the Bible as a book of dos and don'ts. I think it is a picture of the character and nature of God. He still wants to draw close to us, live in us, but sin creates a horrible barrier. This way, we have a book about how to please Him so we can draw near to Him and He to us. He knows we can't possibly follow every little rule and regulation, so He provided for us the blood covering of a sinless, spotless lamb. At first it was an annual event beginning in Egypt, but then it culminated on Golgotha—the place of the skull where He offered His only Son as a complete covering for all the sins of the whole world! He did this because He loves us and just wants to fellowship with us. Now He can without that horrible sin in the way. Jesus, Yeshua is the Messiah of God, the sinless, spotless lamb!

I didn't used to know any of this. Mom and Dad were military. We were raised in the military. We moved all the time because Dad got orders. It never occurred to me to question or object or even complain. They were simply orders and we obeyed. It made for a lonely, dysfunctional childhood. I struggled to make friends, was always the new kid on the block, and never fit in. As a teenager, I discovered the easiest way to fit in was to party and do drugs. Druggies didn't care who you were, where you came from, or what you believed as long as you maintained a steady supply of drugs so everyone could party and get high. I finally had friends.

Things progressed from weekend parties to staying high most of the time and selling drugs to make money and keep the supply going. I wasn't really happy, but I wasn't bored either, and being bored was for me the worst thing in the whole world! It was then, and pretty much still is, very difficult for me to just sit and relax. I have to have something to do. In those days, getting in trouble kept me pretty busy!

I was partying with a gang of bikers one night when the leader of the biker gang did something that made me very angry. Little 'ol skinny me proceeded to chew out this 200-plus pound biker in front of his whole gang! If I had been in my right mind at the time, I would have thought better of it, but I managed to do a pretty good job of putting my foot right in my mouth! In the midst of this rip roaring party, you could have heard a pin drop. I realized then what I had done, but it was too late to retract the words. Suddenly, a Presence entered the room. I didn't see anyone, but I felt it (Later I would realize it was the Presence of the Lord). The gang leader looked me and apologized for what he had done. In front of all his guys, he apologized! I accepted his apology and shortly thereafter left the party in one piece.

One of the times that we received a shipment of five hundred kilos of marijuana, instead of paying our supplier, my boyfriend spent the money. This was bad, very bad! These guys were going to come looking for us, and it would not be pretty! We moved. We really had no choice. We either had to come up with a lot of money very fast or pay the consequences. Unfortunately, we had to move often to either stay one step ahead of the law or one step ahead of disgruntled customers! Now that I look back on it, it was a miserable way to live!

I'm not going into further detail about those days except to say that most of my friends ended up dead or in jail. I sincerely hoped and prayed that the rest somehow met Jesus like I did. This chapter is not about how much trouble I got into, but it is about B'resheet—God breathing life into one of His creations and abiding in that creation. It is about new beginnings. I had sunk about as low as an individual can get, but God!

I met Yeshua on the 17 day of Nisan on the Jewish calendar during the Jesus movement of the 1970s. It was three days after the Passover- a genuine firstfruits resurrection. I was, as they say, a dead man walking until my Messiah breathed new life into me! It was the most profoundly radical turning point of my entire life! "Yeshua said to her, 'I a.m. the Resurrection and the Life! Whoever puts his trust in me will live, even if he dies'" (John 11:25, CJB).

It seemed at the time like a "suddenly," but it really was a divine setup that I fell into. I really wasn't looking for God. At least I didn't think I was. I don't recall thinking that "if there was a God" or "I wonder if there is a God." I considered myself an atheist. I didn't believe in anything I could not connect to with my five senses. I certainly couldn't see, hear, touch, smell, or taste God, so I assumed He didn't really exist. School taught evolution as though it were fact and not a theory, so I figured we were all just one big accident. The way people responded to one another, especially the "good" people, the accident theory made sense to me. I just never gave the whole Supreme Being thing much thought.

I was going about my life as usual when a friend moved into the same apartment complex that I lived in, just two doors down from me. Naturally, I would drop in to visit her from time to time. Every time I did, I could tell she was very excited about something. She would flip open a book called *The Late Great Planet Earth* by some guy named Hal Lindsey[3] and read about how the world was going to end. Then she would open the Bible to the passages of scripture that corresponded to what she had just read. (I later came to find those in the book of Revelation.) She would then proceed to read out of the Bible to me. This was not some passing fancy with her; she really believed this stuff. This didn't just happen from time to time; it happened *every* time I went to visit her!

After a few weeks of this, I decided to put an end to it. I came to the decision that since I really didn't know anything about religion, I would research the major religions so I would have a rebuttal prepared for her. She was definitely fixated on this stuff and needed to broaden her horizons! I got some books on all the major "isms," bought a Bible, and started to read.

Then something strange happened. Every time I started to read about any of the other religions, I would fall asleep! It didn't matter what time of day or night it was, whether I was rested or tired, as I started to read, the next thing I knew, I was asleep! However, when I picked up the Bible I was wide awake. I read it voraciously like something in me was starving, and

I needed to devour as much of it as I possibly could. It was even the old King James Version! So back and forth I went, either reading, reading, reading or sleeping, sleeping, sleeping!

Then it happened. I was in my room reading that Bible when suddenly it hit me like a ton of bricks. God was for real! Yeshua was really the Messiah! This book I was reading was no ordinary book. It was as though Someone stepped into my room and threw all the light switches on! This was the biggest wow, the greatest rush I had ever had, and I had a lot of rushes in my life! I intuitively knew that I needed to do something with this new revelation but had no idea how radically my life was about to change.

I spoke with my girlfriend the next day. I was the perfect picture of "cool." I just simply stated that I thought I would like to go to church with her on Sunday. She said that I probably should buy a dress since the nightclub clothes I wore would be inappropriate for church. I said okay, and we went shopping. I said nothing of my experience of the night before. Sunday I went to church, and then Wednesday night I went back to church. I went every Sunday and Wednesday thereafter.

Eventually I quit going to the bars, drinking, and getting high. My wardrobe gradually changed, even though the church people said nothing about my very short cutoffs and midriff tops! One by one, most of my old party friends drifted away, and all I had left was church friends. The most immediate change was my language. I used to swear worse than most sailors!

Instantly and immediately the swearing was gone. Those words didn't even enter my thoughts!

I did not suffer any drug withdrawals. I didn't have to force myself to quit. I just didn't feel like drinking or doing drugs anymore. What used to be enjoyable was now irritating. I looked forward to going to church and new believer's class. I enjoyed going out with my new friends for ice cream. It's like I was in a waking dream. A whole new life was unfolding before me, and I wasn't sure how or why it was happening, but I liked it! I had friends who didn't drink or do drugs, and I wasn't bored!

The pastor said I needed to be baptized in water. I didn't understand why, but I said okay. Then he said I needed the baptism in the Holy Spirit. I didn't know what that was or why I needed it, but again I said okay. At first, nothing happened, but I figured eventually something would. I was in the honeymoon phase, but I didn't know it. I would ask for things in Jesus's name, and He would actually do them!

At that time, I drove an old classic car that needed some work. Suffice it to say that every time I put fuel in it, it also drank a quart of oil. One time I couldn't get the oil cap off no matter how hard I tried. Then I said, "In the name of Jesus loosen!" It slid off so easily, I fell back on my butt!

One Sunday, a ministry group came to our church from Christ for the Nations Bible Institute in Dallas, Texas. I understood that it was a Bible college, and since I was still in college, I thought it would be nice to go there. After all, most of the people at my church had been Christians for years and knew lots about the Bible, and I couldn't even find the scripture references! The very first scriptures I had ever read were when I bought that old King James Version and started to read a few months earlier. I happened to mention to the assistant pastor in passing that I might like to go there. I'm not really sure how it all happened, but the next thing I knew, I had quit my job, packed all my earthly possessions in my car, and was on my way to Dallas, Texas!

I didn't understand what was happening to me, but God knew! He knew that the honeymoon phase was about to end and the devil, the enemy of our souls, was about to unleash his stinking lies on me. I didn't have a clue, but He knew and He hid me under the shadow of His wings in a faraway place where I couldn't get drugs so easily when discouragement moved in. When the flashbacks started from all the LSD I had taken, someone was there with discernment to deliver me.

By the time I left Christ for the Nations Institute, I was clean. My eyes were no longer two slits but were wide open. I was no longer skin and bones from too many drugs and not enough food. I really and truly was a new creation! I don't remember learning a lot about the Bible while I was there—that would come later primarily through personal study, research, and reading the many excellent books available to us today. What I did learn was how to live a changed life. What I received there was much more valuable than an education. It was God's halfway house transitioning me from the old life into the new.

I made a lot of assumptions in those early days about church and Christians. I assumed that everyone in church had a real-live born-again testimony, that Christians all loved and accepted each other, that everyone was baptized in the Holy Spirit with the evidence of speaking in tongues or that they wanted to be. Boy, did I have a lot to learn!

Jewish in the Gentile Church

I was born Jewish, but I wasn't raised Jewish. The Holocaust pretty much sealed that. Mom was raised Orthodox Jewish. She already struggled with some of the religious issues such as women being separated from the men and treated as second-class citizens. Everything was in Hebrew, a language she didn't know and wasn't encouraged to learn. Her picture of God was framed by religion; there was no relationship. The thread was thin and frayed that held her to her roots; it could have been snipped with a scissors. The Holocaust severed it with an ax.

Mom's favorite mantra was "If God really existed and we are His chosen people, how could He have allowed the Holocaust to happen?" She was also fond of reciting the Shema during our discussions about God: "Hear, O Israel! The LORD is our God, the LORD is one!" (Deuteronomy 6:4, NASB). Mom knew some things about religion, but nothing about relationship.

I am of the firm opinion that people believe what they want to believe. God had the answers if Mom wanted to know them. She wanted to nurse her anger and bitterness about life's injustices. She suffered a lot of life's injustices as a child and went through many highs and lows as an adult. She lost a child, then lost her husband. I don't ever recall Mom thanking God for the blessings, but she did blame Him for the losses.

I've read some of the things rabbis have written about life's injustices, the Holocaust, and Jesus as Messiah. They, too, operate under a finite understanding (as do all of us) of who God really is. Some of them teach that because we are God's chosen people and agreed to the covenant, we are held to a higher standard—bound by the blessings and curses of Deuteronomy 28. We first abandoned God, over and over again, so then He abandoned us.

I did tell Mom that because God is God, He can be who He wants to be and do what He wants to do. He does not need our approval. If He happens to exist in three persons (the Elohiym, Genesis 1:26) and have seven Spirits (Revelations 3:1), He does not have to explain it all to us nor ask our permission. He said "I AM WHO I AM" (Exodus 3:14a, NASB). That should pretty much settle it for us.

The scriptures are filled with references, types, and pictures of His Messiah. In my opinion, these are extremely difficult to miss unless one chooses not to believe. I've heard some rabbis teach that when Abraham took Isaac up to mount Moriah, that he made a mistake and God had to stop him from sacrificing his son. I think we need to stretch our imaginations here. Abraham had a pretty good track record of hearing from God. What if everything that happened was supposed to happen just as it did? What if this was a seed sown into the very ground that centered around the conflict of good versus evil, deity versus the demonic? What if it's a type, a shadow, a picture of Isaiah 53, a Messiah that was really supposed to be our Passover Lamb instead of an all-powerful deliverer from Roman oppression? Why else would God have us celebrate the Passover year after year? Why did we have to celebrate our deliverance from slavery by the slaying of an innocent lamb? Could it be that God was painting an extraordinary picture for human eyes to see that the devil, immersed in his cesspool of evil, could not begin to fathom? God is so far beyond anything we can imagine, so why do we keep trying to put Him into our little religious boxes? Absurd!

When I came to the realization that Yeshua really was the Messiah, there were very few Jews who believed as I did. Most Jews were of the opinion that to believe that Yeshua was really our Messiah constituted treason of the highest order! To some, I became as though I were dead. To others, I had simply converted to Christianity and was no longer a Jew. (Tell *that* to all the Jews who converted to Christianity during the Holocaust but perished in the death camps anyway!) It's always amazed me that a Jew can believe in eastern religion, new age, or even be atheistic and still be Jewish, but believe in Yeshua as Messiah and that's it! It's all over! Seems to me like the devil doesn't want us to know the truth. Anyway, just to set the record straight, I didn't convert to anything. I'm still a Jew. I will always be Jewish; I just happen to believe that Yeshua really is our Messiah.

So there I was, not really wanted by my family and abandoned by all my old friends. I made some new friends in the Gentile church I attended, but I was very careful not to reveal my Jewish heritage to anyone. I had seen some prejudice by Gentiles toward Jews and didn't want to ruin the new relationships I was developing.

As it turned out that was one of the few areas of wisdom that I managed to fall into early in my walk with the Lord. I was exposed to some very interesting preaching in those early years. I heard all about how the Jews were the ones who crucified Jesus. (Funny, I thought it was all of our sin and need for redemption that put Him there.) I also heard that since we screwed up and refused to believe in Him as a people, that God was done with us, our covenant was forever broken, and the church replaced us as "spiritual Israel." I also heard that we *deserved* all the persecutions we went through!

What kind of nonsense is *that*!? The *real* Israel is not made up of Gentile Christians but Jews. What other nation has risen from the ashes after almost two thousand years? Our God does *not* break covenant, and I'm pretty sure that all the Christians who "were stoned, sawed in two, murdered by the sword; they went about clothed in sheepskins and goatskins, destitute, persecuted, mistreated, wandering about in deserts and mountains, living in caves and holes in the ground! The world was not worthy of them!" (Hebrews 11:37–38, CJB) did not deserve persecution either!

I would have to guess that those Gentiles who believe that they have replaced the Jews as spiritual Israel have never read Leviticus 26. Verse 44 pretty much sums it up: "Yet in spite of this, when they are in the land of their enemies, I will not reject them, nor will I so abhor them as to destroy them, breaking My covenant with them; for I am the Lord their God" (Leviticus 26:44, NASB).

I'm glad to say that I haven't heard any of that kind of preaching in several years. Some Gentile churches are even attempting to get in touch with their Hebraic roots! These have been greatly influenced by some of my favorite teachers such as Perry Stone[4], Chuck Pierce[5], and Rabbi Curt Landry[6]. I've always thought that it would be much better for the church, both Jew and Gentile, to celebrate the Jewish festivals such as Passover and Hanukkah rather than festivals of pagan origin like Easter and Christmas. Just saying…

I've often wished I could attend a church or synagogue made up primarily of Jewish believers (Messianic Jews), so I would feel like I fit in someplace, but that never worked out. Better yet, how about a church made up of a number of both Jews and Gentiles? Now that would be something! Maybe someday.

The enemy crafted a masterful plan to erect and keep in place the dividing wall between Jew and Gentile, but it seems like there is some glimmer of hope that it might finally be dissolving a little. One can only hope and dream that it will be so.

In the meantime, I attended Gentile churches pretending to be one of them. That worked for me at least for a season.

Cancer

Cancer. It's an ominous word filled with dread and fear, lots of fear. I'd heard this word spoken in times past over others. I knew from reading nursing journals and textbooks that one's survival depended on the stage of the cancer and the rate of growth of the tumor(s). I read that once a person was cancer-free for five years, they were considered to be "cured". I also read that many persons were official "cancer survivors."

Personally, I didn't know anyone who had survived cancer. It didn't seem to matter if they were young or old, male or female, rich or poor. They had all died. My dad made it ten months. His thirty-six-year-old sister was dying from cancer. In the years to come, my mom, another uncle, my sister-in-law, and many friends would succumb to this horrible plague.

I also knew that the available treatments for cancer in 1988 were as bad as the disease leaving its victims weak, nauseated, and debilitated. Many people I had talked to were so sick from the side effects they simply lost the will to live. They just wanted it to be over with.

My own story began before the actual diagnosis. I like to get alone with God in January of each year to hear from Him about the upcoming year. Some friends of mine had a retreat center that was snowed in. It was a perfect place to "hibernate" for the week! I spent that week in fasting and prayer. The Lord said nothing about the upheaval that was about to descend upon me.

He talked about faith. I looked out the window to the beautiful view of the mountains where I was. There were pine trees, snow, and a small building on the adjacent mountainside. Suddenly, fog began to move in. It covered the mountain like a thick blanket within a matter of minutes. Then the Lord began to talk to me. He said, "Daughter, what do you see"? I replied, "Nothing but fog." Then He inquired, "What is really there"? I answered "A mountainside with trees, snow, and a small building." He then said to me in that still, small, gentle voice that I'd grown to love: "Faith is like that. What you see is fog, but there is so much more that is really there. When I ask you to believe for something, you can't see it yet, but I know what is real—what's really there. If you can simply agree with My reality, when the time is right, I will clear the fog. Many times, My people believe there is nothing there, so they go on their way and miss what I have for them."

I was having some "female symptoms." Nothing significant—I'd had female symptoms before. I usually went to the MD, got a prescription, and no more symptoms! This time was different. I went to the doctor, and he referred me to a specialist. That's when I got the dreaded diagnosis. It was no longer something that happened to other people. It had happened to me.

The gynecologist went over my options. He said the cancer was advanced and maybe had already spread. He said that I would need to have a radical hysterectomy and that he didn't do them. I would need a specialized specialist; someone who specialized in female cancers. He had tears in his eyes! I could see it on his face! He was giving me up for dead already! He made me an appointment.

I then went to my pastor to tell him and ask him for prayer and he cried! This is not good! I needed some words of encouragement, some warriors on my team, and all I got were tears! This couldn't be happening, not now, not to me. I had just, the month before, spent a week alone with God in prayer and fasting! Why didn't He tell me? Why didn't He just heal me then?

Thoughts began to race through my overloaded brain. I had just started my nursing career two and a half years earlier—the very career that the Lord had directed me into! What am I going to do? Who's going to raise my five-year-old son? None of my relatives belonged to Jesus. The boy's biological father was an ex-con who had spent most of his adult life in and out of jail. My son would probably end up living with a sister who didn't even believe God existed!

Then I began to think about the promises God had given me. He had already told me I was going to the foreign field someday as a missionary. My first ever short-term missions' trip was scheduled for that very year!

I also began to think of the Christians I had known who had battled cancer. Some of them believed that all they had to do was claim their healing in Jesus's name, and it was a done deal. Somehow if they were able to muster up enough faith, God would miraculously heal them. He *had* to! Most of these died of cancer. "Name it and claim it" either didn't work or had some serious flaws in the theology. Something had to be missing because His Word promised healing!

I looked up healing scriptures. Psalm 107:20 states, "He sent his word and healed them, he delivered them from destruction" (CJB). This verse is neither about the innocent nor the righteous. It is about foolish people who suffered affliction because of their sins (verse 17)! Jeremiah 17:14 says: "Heal me, Adonai, and I will be healed; save me, and I will be saved, for you are my praise" (CJB). Verse 13 says of the Lord, "All who abandon you will be ashamed, those who leave you will be inscribed in the dust, because they have abandoned Adonai, the source of living water" (Jeremiah 17:13, CJB). I certainly had no intentions of abandoning the Lord. After all, where else would I go? To whom would I turn to if not Him?

I remembered that one of the reasons He hung on that cross for us, became the Passover lamb for us, was to carry away not only our sin, but also all our diseases (Isaiah 53:5). Even before His sacrifice on the cross, *everyone* who came to Him was healed. He healed them all!

Where was the key? How could I lay hold of the healing I so desperately needed? I went to prayer. I reminded God of all the things He had promised me over the years that had not been fulfilled. I reminded

Him I had a son to raise. I listed for Him all the reasons why I should be healed (as if He didn't already know them)! I heard nothing. No promise of a supernatural healing, no battle plan to defeat the enemy, no "anointed" man or woman of the Lord that I should have pray over me, anointing me with oil (James 5:14).

I came to the end of myself and with a deep sigh remembered that I was bought and paid for with a precious price and that I was not my own (1 Corinthians 7:23). I relinquished my so-called right to live in this body and said to God: "I belong to you. You are the master. I am the servant. If you wish to heal me, that would be awesome! If you wish to take me home to yourself to heaven, I trust your decision. I know you will take care of my son, for he is yours also." After all, His Word says in Philippians 3:10–11: "That I may know Him and the power of His resurrection and the fellowship of His sufferings, being conformed to His death; in order that I may attain to the resurrection from the dead" (NASB). If I was going to have resurrection power, I was going to have to die! When I finished praying that prayer, that's when I heard His voice.

"Daughter, I want you to go to the doctors and whatever they tell you to do, do it. Do not worry about the medical expenses. I will make $10,000 as though it were one dollar. As you intercede over your body, I Myself will set boundaries around the cancer so that it cannot spread."

That's not exactly what I wanted to hear. I was hoping for a supernatural healing so I could avoid the pain and agony of surgery. I did not have any health insurance

SOSHANA GOLDBERG

at the time, so the expense was definitely an issue! I had heard someone teach that the Hebrew word for intercession, paga, held several meanings one of which was to set boundaries. Strong's says that it literally means to impinge, often violently[7]. Well, I intended to impinge violently, big time, in prayer on this cancer! One thing I did understand was that I had to be obedient to the Lord in *every* area of His instruction. I could not afford to pick and choose which part to obey and which part not to. Disobedience simply was not an option!

I went to work. The doctor scheduled me for surgery in two weeks. He said that at that time, he would mark me for radiation therapy. I began to intercede. I looked up every biblical promise I could find on healing, wrote them down, and declared them over my body daily for the whole two weeks! I told the devil that he was a lair and that I was *not* going to die but live and praise *My God* in the land of the living! I refused to allow fear or discouragement get me down. The devil tried to remind me that everyone in my family line that had cancer died from it. I quoted the scriptures and the Word of the Lord to him. The devil bombarded my mind with fears of every kind, but I leaned into the Lord my God, quoted His Word, and trusted in His promises.

I'm not going to lie and say that I didn't feel any fear during this two-week waiting period. The enemy assailed me with fear daily. I just refused to agree with it. This blanket of fear was like the fog—my healing was being hidden by it, but from God's perspective, the healing was more real than the fog of fear. That fog would soon be dissipated completely from my life!

◀ 34 ▶

I went in for the surgery, and when I came out of the anesthesia, I was in more pain than I had ever experienced in my whole life! I should have thrown in some prayer for post-op pain reduction! I had always been told that childbirth was one of the most painful events one would experience in life. Whoever came up with *that* tidbit of information had never had a radical hysterectomy! I spent six days in the hospital and six weeks recovering. I was extremely weak. I had never gone through anything like that and never wanted to go through it again!

As soon as I woke up from the anesthesia, my doctor informed me that the surgery went very well, but that the tumor was poorly differentiated. They had tried to get it all, but it would be impossible to know until all the tissue biopsies came back. That would take three more days. He said then they could target the radiation therapy to hopefully kill any remaining cancer cells.

The next three days went by in a blur of pain, fatigue, and emotion. I was too tired to fight anymore, but at least I knew my pastor would be praying for me. The morning of the third day dawned. I don't remember if it was sunny or raining. It didn't matter. I just wanted to know what the test results were and what was going to come next. After all, the Lord just said to do what the doctors said to do. He didn't say how involved that would end up being.

My doctor entered the room. He said that the test results were all negative. It looked like there was no spread, and I would not need radiation therapy after all! Praise the Name of the Lord most high who delivers us out of all destructions! Praise His Holy name! The doctor did say I would need frequent checkups over the next five years to make sure I would stay cancer-free, but I knew deep within my spirit that the Lord had indeed placed boundaries round about that cancer so that it could not spread! I was healed! It's been well over twenty-four years now, and I can truly say that His Word will not return void (Isaiah 55:11)!

In addition to all that, somehow I qualified for some program that allowed the hospital to write off my entire bill. I still had a few smaller expenses to pay off, but He did indeed make $10,000 as though it was a dollar!

Now all I had to do was trust Him to provide for the upcoming missions trip to Jamaica! That would be peanuts compared to what He had just done in my life!

The Lord Yeshua, my Messiah, had just walked me through what would be one of the biggest battles of my life. He taught me how to wage war against all the thoughts that the enemy had bombarded my mind with. He carried me through the emotional highs and lows that I would experience. He especially taught me to trust in Him explicitly. He knew I would need these lessons for the road of life that awaited me.

Marriage

I've been married most of my adult life. The first time was for seven years to an unbeliever who had no intention of ever walking with the Lord or even legally within the society to which he was born in. It was birthed in iniquity and ended in disaster.

The second time has been for well over twenty years to a God-fearing man who loves the Lord. You'd think that after all this I'd be an expert on marriage with fountains of wisdom on being a godly wife and mother. Unfortunately, I still haven't figured it out, but that's for another chapter!

I have a one-track mind. A lot of psychologists and sociologists have expounded on the differences between men and women. They claim that women are much better at multitasking than men. Somewhere en route to this life, I missed the female multitasking line! (I think I got sidetracked by the archery demonstration.)

Somehow, I always thought that once married, a person was supposed to pursue their life's work and passion for the things of God. Marriage was supposed to take care of itself. Everyone should just calmly and logically discuss issues as they arise. As new information

SOSHANA GOLDBERG

is gathered and disseminated, rational decisions could be made. After all, covenant was cut and that means until death do us part. Apparently, this was a faulty assumption on my part in both marriages.

I assumed that my first marriage failed because we were extremely unequally yoked. I decided that I was fully capable of raising my young son on my own and didn't really need to be married. I even told God I didn't want to get married ever again! I had been through enough and figured the Lord would understand. I was, once again, wrong! I wasn't aware in my current level of Christian immaturity that one should never say never to God!

Life was full, and I was busy working and raising a child. A lot of my time was spent volunteering at the local church. I had just completed my first mission's trip and had learned so much in preparation for the life that the Lord was calling me to.

Earlier that year, Jesus had healed me of cancer, paid for my medical expenses, and provided the finances for this missions' trip. I was on a spiritual mountaintop and was definitely *not* looking for a husband! I wanted to be a missionary and seemed well on my way to getting there.

People often ask me how I met my husband. I smile in anticipation of the look on their faces as I tell them I met him at my ex-mother-in-law's house. Yes, you heard me right. I purposely avoided singles groups at church. The only time I was in mixed company was at work (where I was all business) or at church (where I was all spiritual)! It was Christmas morning, and I took

◀ 38 ▶

my son to his grandma's house to get his presents. My future husband was there to take my ex-mother-in-law to church for Christmas service. I had heard about this guy—that he would run errands for her and repair things around the house, and she would prepare home-cooked meals for him. I never thought much about their relationship.

I'm not sure exactly what happened next. I'm usually quiet around strangers until I get to know them a little bit and figure out if they can be trusted or not. This time I just couldn't quit talking! I told him of my passion for the Lord and my desire to be a missionary. We visited for a while, and then we all went to church together. I didn't see him again for a couple of months and didn't think much about it. Apparently, cupid's arrow struck firm and fast in him, though, and he thought *a lot* about me.

Suddenly, it seemed like every time I took my son to his grandma's, this man was there. We began to spend more time together. Then one day, he said he had picked up a pamphlet where a couple were not sure if they should get married or not, so they fasted and prayed. He didn't ask me to marry him; he asked me to fast and pray! Well, as an intercessor, fasting and praying was my thing! I said of course I would fast and pray. Somehow I managed to miss the part about getting married. In prayer, the Lord said, "You will not run from this man. I am putting you together for wholeness." I was stunned. How did all this sneak up on me? I knew enough to know that I had better obey the Lord. Every time in the past when I didn't, I really lived to regret it!

After the one-day fast, we met up and he asked me what the Lord said. I told him. He said that the Lord said yes to him as well and just like that we were engaged! I was in shock but determined to obey God in this. I enjoyed seeing this guy and very much liked his company, but marriage? I trusted the Lord enough to know that He had my best in mind and everything would be okay.

That's when life got really bizarre. My ex-husband really never had much to do with us. My son visited him on occasion, but he didn't support his kid. He barely had enough money to support himself! Suddenly he decided he didn't want me to remarry. He didn't want me, but he didn't want anyone else to have me either! He threatened to kill us and take the kid. He started following both me and my fiancé around. He would sit in his car and watch when I went to work. He walked all around my fiancé's house presumably looking for a way to break in. The police were well acquainted with him and all the goings-on but seemed powerless to stop him.

That's when things got even weirder. I got up one morning to go to work when there was a knock on my door. The neighbor said my car was on fire! I looked outside and the whole interior of my car was black. Smoke was coming out of the windows! I called the fire department, and then called my fiancé. He said he'd be right over.

When they put out the fire, the stereo was gone. They said it was arson. I knew it was my ex. Then I talked to my fiancé, and he said that he would be delayed in coming. Someone had tried to torch his pickup, but it was so airtight that only the dash and air conditioning was melted. He was able to rewire his pickup and drove to my apartment. I couldn't afford to buy another car, so my fiancé made sure I got to work, church, and everywhere else I needed to go. We all knew, including the police, who was responsible for the arsons, but they couldn't prove a thing.

I interceded and prayed hedges of protection around us daily. God gave me promises from His word. The Lord said my land would be married (Isaiah 62:4). My favorite was Psalm 37:10: "Soon the wicked will be no more; you will look for his place, and he won't be there" (cjb). This was a test, and I knew the Lord would deliver us and give us a testimony!

I had peace, but my fiancé was definitely stressed. He was only two years old in the Lord and was used to "taking care of business." Waiting was *not* something he was interested in doing! He did, however, prove himself faithful. He could have just walked away from the mess and the stress, but he didn't. Instead he manned up and stuck with me and my son. He needed to see the goodness and faithfulness of God, and I needed to see that when the going gets tough, some men don't run.

One day in prayer, the Lord told me that there would be one more test and then it would be finished. The test came about a week later. My fiancé went out to his pickup to come get me and take me to work. When he opened the door, urine flowed out—a *lot* of urine. My ex lived in a little camp trailer and apparently had emptied his holding tank into the pickup!

Once again we had a mess to deal with. More police reports were filed. I got a ride with my neighbor to my fiancé's apartment, and we began the cleanup process. There was urine floating in the floor. It had saturated the seat and glove compartment. Everything was soaked. We put the car seat cover in vinegar to soak and proceeded to bleach all the plastic and metal. We threw away the papers from the glove box. Then we removed the seat so we could soak it in vinegar and clean underneath it.

That's when the miracle took place. That's when the grace of God became fully manifested to us. My fiancé had an old worn King James Bible that he kept under the driver's seat down in the well. There was urine in the well, but an inch around the Bible was completely dry. He picked up the Bible, and it was totally dry. He handed it to me, and I smelled it. There was the familiar smell of old parchment, but no smell of urine anywhere! Is there anything too hard for our God! After everything was said and done, all that came out of this last attack was a much cleaner pickup! Praise to His glorious name!

That was, indeed, the last attack. We were married in the little church that the Lord had called me to when He first called me to be an intercessor. The church provided the building and the food, and I borrowed the wedding dress. We had to buy a few flowers and a cake. We didn't have any money for a honeymoon until we opened all the cards at the reception. *Then* we had more than enough! We actually made money getting married!

After we came home, my new husband had a job offer in another state, so we packed up and moved, starting a whole new life together. So what about the ex? Oh yea, he was going to follow us but managed to get in a shoot-out with someone who supposedly owed him some money, and they both ended up in jail. We never saw him again.

> When I am afraid, I will put my trust in You. In God, whose word I praise, in God I have put my trust; I shall not be afraid. What can mere man do to me?
>
> Psalm 56:3–4 (NASB)

A Gift of Faith

I never understood how a gift of faith worked before this. I had faith and believed God for some extraordinary things, but never like this.

My dream of becoming a missionary was finally coming true! Both my husband and I had quit our jobs, sold most of our possessions, and had completed missions training with YWAM (Youth with a Mission). We had already spent three weeks in the newly liberated Russia of the early 1990s, evangelizing, putting on dramas, and praying deliverance for those recently saved.

Russia was a real eye-opener. We knew the culture would be different, but it is truly amazing how much of our own culture and belief systems we still projected onto the Russian people. We assumed the people would largely be atheistic. That simply was not true. Many were still deeply rooted in the Christian Orthodox Church. Joseph Stalin[8] was involved in the occult and drew much of the population into it with him. Bibles were few and far between, but Ouija boards, tarot cards, crystal balls, and other similar paraphernalia were common. We knew these people would need salvation and healing, but they *really* needed deliverance!

We felt like the Lord was calling us to return to Russia full time. We didn't, however, have the money as we had spent everything on missions training and our previous trip to Russia. We simply believed God. He said we were returning to Russia, so it was up to Him to provide. We made the plane reservations and had perfect peace while doing so. There was some time before we had to pay for the tickets, and we had some itinerating to do, so we figured in the course of our travels God would lay on someone's heart to provide for the trip.

Sometimes I wish things would just go smoothly and easily, but it seems like they never do. The devil already had a counterattack planned to keep us from going! My mom had just returned from a trip back east to visit her brother. One of her legs had swollen while she was there, so she went to the doctor and was diagnosed with cancer! Then, my husband got a call that his dad was also diagnosed with cancer and was scheduled for surgery. Here we were, having already quit our jobs, traveling the country trying to raise support to return to Russia as missionaries, and we get not one, but two bad reports! But God!

We prayed and both of us really felt like we were to plan on going to Russia anyway. God would take care of our parents. My husband's dad had the surgery, recovered, and did remarkably well. He lived to a ripe old age without any further cancer. My mom started chemotherapy. The doctors were optimistic concerning her outcome.

We finished itinerating and had raised enough monthly support to go, but no plane ticket money yet. The due date arrived. We either had to pay for the tickets or cancel. We believed that we were not supposed to go into debt for this, that God had called and He would provide. Then came the phone call! The pastor of the church that was sending us out called to tell us that a man in the church whom we had never met walked up to the pastor and gave him a check for $2,000 and said this is for the couple going to Russia! It was exactly what we needed when we needed it! Hallelujah! Praise the name of the Lord!

About six months went by and the ministry was going well. My mom had completed the chemotherapy and the tumor had shrunk, but then it came back larger than ever. The doctors scheduled her for radiation. They had lost their initial enthusiasm for her cure but felt that the radiation would buy her at least a couple of years. I made the decision to visit her over my birthday. Mom had never asked Yeshua to be her Messiah, so this was foremost in my mind as I made the plane reservations.

Getting in and out of Russia is never an easy proposition. You don't just show them your passport, get on a plane, and leave. You have to have the proper documents and visas. Everything takes time—a lot of time. In the early 1990s, all international flights went through Moscow. There was no other route in or out of Russia by air. I set about to make the necessary arrangements—a flight reservation to Moscow and another one from Moscow to the United States. My passport went to the authorities for visa approval. I was told it would take about three weeks for everything to come together, and I had a month—no problem, right? Wrong!

Late Saturday evening I received a call from one of my sisters. She informed me that mom was in renal failure and had three to five *days* to live! What happened! I thought I had plenty of time! Mom wasn't even saved yet! This can't possibly be happening! What can I do?

I went immediately to prayer. I told the Lord I needed *several* miracles *right now*! I asked Him to help me get out of Russia as quickly as possible, give me favor with the airlines so I can get my flights changed, special favor with the government office where my passport was so I could get my visa approval, keep Mom alive until I got there, bring her to salvation in Yeshua, and make me to know that I know that she is saved! No problem, right? All in a day's work for our Lord!

I called Scandinavian Air, and they were awesome! They said that whenever I needed to get out of Moscow, just let them know and I would be on a plane for the United States. I called Aeroflot—the Russian airline. This would not be so easy. They had one spot on a flight Monday afternoon to Moscow. I told them I would be on it. I still had no way of knowing if I could get my passport and visa that quickly—that would be the *real* miracle. I called Tatiana, our liaison with them. She didn't see any way possible I could get it Monday morning. All I could do was wait. Somehow I had that peace beyond all understanding that everything would work out all right.

morning. None of the local ministers I called would preach a funeral on Sunday afternoon, so I got to share the message of salvation with my whole unbelieving family at one time! I told them that Mom was in heaven and wanted to eventually see them all there too. Talk about a captive audience! Someone might get up and walk out of a church service, but who's going to walk out on a funeral?

One of the best things about the whole experience was the peace and assurance that everything I asked for would be accomplished regardless of what the enemy tried to pull. When someone operates in a gift of faith, the enemy does not stand a chance! There's no room for doubt—you just know! I wish I could always operate in a gift of faith, but as time would progress, God had many other things to teach me that would not come so easily.

Missionary?

For me, who I am and what I do for a living are two separate things. Most of my life I've made a living as a nurse, but that is not who I really am. I believe that each one of us has a prophetic destiny breathed into us by the Lord. God has a plan for our lives (Jeremiah 29:11). His plan is perfect, it's designed to fit our personality and desires, and it's exciting!

The problem, as I see it, is that most people have their own plan and aren't really interested in God's plan. The enemy lies to them and tells them that they won't like God's plan as well as their own, that God does not really want them to have fun, or that God's plan will make their life difficult and filled with poverty. They don't really know God or His Word very well, so they attempt to make their way in life the best they know how. Things happen and they figure that's just life or that God is out to get them, doesn't care about them, or really love them.

As a child, I never really wanted to be a nurse. I wanted to be a marine biologist, but little did I know in my youthful inexperience that the adventure the Lord had planned for me would take me places that as a nurse

I could always find employment, but if I had become a marine biologist I would never be able to work. So I went to nursing school at the Lord's request. I was told that no one ever got accepted the first year they applied—I did. It was the most work-intensive school experience of my life! My mind was still not completely healed from all the drugs, but the Lord enabled me to graduate in the top of my class with a 4.0 GPA!

What I thought I *really* wanted to be was a foreign missionary. I figured that nursing would be a good background for missions' work. I didn't know any missionaries personally or any nurses for that matter, but it just seemed like it would work. Practically, I didn't really know what missionaries did except to go places where no one had heard the gospel, try to fit in with the local population, and share Jesus with them.

In the 1980s, there were only a handful of "acceptable" occupations for persons in full-time ministry. There was a huge gulf between what was considered ministry and laity. If you were part of the laity and you wanted to minister, you were supposed to work in the nursery or Sunday school, be an usher, clean the church, or care for the sick. If you were a minister, you were expected to attend Bible college, get ordained by an accepted ministry organization, and be a pastor, teacher, or evangelist *if* you were a man. If you were woman, you were either on the worship team or you were screwed! It was easier in those days as a woman to be a doctor or a lawyer than to be a minister! Some women, however, had made it as missionaries and were even accepted by the church as legitimate ministers! Since I could not carry a tune in a bag, hence, no worship team for me, the logical choice was missionary. All I knew was that I wanted to serve God, no matter what! Nothing else was important to me. So I finished nursing school, worked for a few years building some experience, and then went to missions training with Youth with a Mission (YWAM).

My first mission's trip was a short-term trip to Jamaica. Just getting there would be a major challenge! I was weak from major surgery and had no money. I had just fought the most horrendous battle ever over cancer. It would have been very easy to just forget about the missions' trip this year and go another time, but I felt that the Lord really wanted me to go. I decided to submit everything to Him in prayer and trust Him for the finances. Right when I needed to either pay for the trip or opt out, the money came through!

We were to minister to a family camp for our denomination. Our team would be doing some teaching, mentoring, puppets for the kids, and generally just sharing the gospel with them. They were very legalistic in their beliefs, so we went humbly in, adhering to their dress and behavior codes, so we could minister some truth to them about God's wonderful grace. I was very much looking forward to this trip and even had some messages prepared in case I would be asked to teach one of the classes.

God had other plans. The team leader was the pastor of my church. There were a few others from our church as well, but most of the team came from other places so this was the first time we met them. Most of them were young and this was their first missions' trip. Seasoned missionaries we were not!

Sometimes, I just wish the devil would take a vacation, but he just doesn't get it! He could probably use a rest after all these centuries of perpetrating evil, but he just doesn't let up! One of the young ladies on our team had some emotional instability issues that had never surfaced in her home church, but boy did they surface on the mission field! The Lord did not call me to preach or teach on that trip, but He did call me to get up early each morning, walk and pray over the compound, and babysit one very emotionally troubled young girl! If her "issues" had been allowed to surface, it would have destroyed any credibility we would have had with that local church. As it was, we were able to keep a lid on things and send her safely back to her home church without major incident. Our team leader was then free to minister truths about God's grace that these people otherwise would not have received. The devil wanted to keep them bound and did everything he could to do just that!

I persisted in my dream to be a full-time missionary, checking out various training venues and missions' organizations. What I didn't know was that God was calling me to be a prophetic intercessor. I should have figured this out by this time as God would consistently use me to pray into situations, but no one had written books or taught about this as an actual calling. What God was doing through me and asking me to do for Him simply was not recognized in the church at that time. I knew that I had the greatest joy in the prayer closet and seeing prayers answered, but I didn't know anything about it!

My next short-term missions trip was to Russia with YWAM. My husband and I had just finished missions training and our team was going to a place that just a couple years before would have been impossible! The Russian people were so unfamiliar with anything Western, let alone with the Gospel that I think they had more culture shock than we did! We held meetings—large ones where thousands came forward to receive Jesus as their savior. We could never have envisioned anything like this in the USA!

The team leadership did most of the preaching, but we each had opportunities to speak and minister. We performed dramas on the streets drawing large crowds with many more salvations. Jesus was literally adding to the church daily those who would be saved (Acts 2:47). One of the best things for me was that there were four of us ladies who gathered early each morning and prayed for the team and over the days' activities. We would wait on the Lord to see if He had anything specific to say about our ministry for that day. We would then share with the team leadership what we felt the Lord was saying. The leadership was open to what we were hearing and based the day's ministry efforts on the Lord's leading. Everything went more smoothly on this trip than on any other trip we've been on before or since! We felt like we were an important part of the team and not just tag-along missionaries-in-training! I just knew this was what I was made for!

We returned to the States and prepared to be full-time missionaries for as long as the Lord wanted us to be. We itinerated and raised enough money for our monthly expenses, but not for the airfare to return. But God! The Lord provided the airfare exactly when we needed it!

We spent two years living and working in Russia. Mostly, we distributed humanitarian aid from the United States, but we also taught in some of the Bible schools set up by other YWAMers to train the Russian believers to reach and disciple their own people. I loved being in Russia. It took a year to learn enough of the language to get around and to win the trust of the Russians we worked with every day. My husband and I made some of the best friends of our entire lives there in Russia.

The Russian people have been through so much more than we can possibly imagine! They told stories of lying in bed in the middle of the night listening for the elevator because that is when the KGB would come and take friends, relatives, and neighbors away. Most of these were sent to Siberia or disappeared, never be heard from again. Trust was a *big* issue for these people. When we first arrived, they would tell us what they felt we wanted to hear because that is what kept them alive. We got used to being lied to! After the first year was over, something shifted. The very people, who lied to us the year before, became our best friends and most trusted allies. Now they would go to bat for us even if it meant getting up in the middle of the night to do so! I began to realize that Americans had no real concept of being a true friend.

My husband was responsible for finding storage and distribution points for the shipping containers of aid that came from the United States. We would get together and pray for each one, and then my husband would go and talk to various ones about their facilities. Sometimes the Lord would tell him, "This is not the place, just be nice to them, and I will show you the right place." It was very easy to get this stuff stolen by the Russian mafia, but we never lost a single container of goods!

One day, in prayer, the Lord told me to go to Yekaterinburg, in central Russia, and pray over the high places and the places where blood was shed especially where the Czar and his family was killed at the start of the Bolshevik revolution. We lived a long way from there and didn't know anyone in that region. Once one left the more populated areas of western Russia, it was almost impossible to find anyone who spoke English, and we only spoke some broken Russian.

I've always been one to just obey the leading of the Lord without a lot of questioning, so I told my husband about it, we made plane reservations and went. It never occurred to me to wonder how we were going to find these "high" places or where innocent blood was shed. We'd never been to Yekaterinburg, had no map of the area, and no Internet access to look things up. We just went.

When we arrived at the airport, we caught the bus into the city, found a motel, and made reservations. As we left the motel and walked across the street, my husband noticed a taxi parked there and felt we were supposed to talk to that man. We explained as best we could what we were doing and why we were in the city. He grew very excited and animated. He said we should not stay in the motel we had checked into. He wanted us to stay with him! He went into the motel, checked us out, and gave us our money back. He also let us know that he was very familiar with all the places we wanted to go, and he would take us there himself! We had a wonderful three days there staying with the taxi driver and his family and had no problems doing exactly what the Lord wanted us to do! All I can say is when you hear from God, take a step of faith, obey, and the Lord will do the rest!

Did I mention that I loved being in Russia? Sure, there were some hard times, some prayer battles, some testing of our faith, but I felt like I was where I belonged. Then one day my husband said we were to leave and go back to the United States. I had envisioned maybe returning after five or ten years, but we had only been there for two years! I was just starting to get more comfortable with the culture and the language. It could not possibly be time to return already. It was true that in the five or six years since the fall of communism, a lot of Russians had been saved, churches were thriving, and leadership was being trained and raised up, but surely there was much more work to be done that we could be a part of!

I balked at going back. I argued with my husband, but he had heard from God and we were leaving. America was a nation "saying, 'I am rich, I have gotten rich, I don't need a thing!' You don't know that you are the one who is wretched, pitiable, poor, blind and naked!" (Revelations 3:17, CJB). Most of the Russian people we knew had very little in material possessions, but they did have a childlike faith in the Lord that was refreshing. We had seen healings and deliverances in Russia. I could not recall seeing anything close to that in America.

We returned to the land of the free and easy, home of the overfed, complacent church. We were back where I would pray for people who kind of hoped God would answer their prayer but didn't really believe He would and were genuinely shocked on the rare occasion in which He did. I was miserable. I went back to work as a nurse and attended a local church but never felt welcomed there.

It took me a whole year to realize that God really did want us back in the States, that He really did speak to my husband, and that I was the one holding up the show! He revealed to me that I had given place to a spirit of discouragement because I didn't really trust my husband to hear from God and ultimately hadn't trusted God to use my situation to place me where and when He wanted me to be!

When we allow a spirit of discouragement to come in, it strips us of our courage, takes our spiritual armor away from us, and leaves us ineffective. God was waiting patiently for me to get re-armored for the next phase of our lives, the next battles that would prove to be much more intense than anything we had ever faced before, but I didn't see any of it until I repented for my stinking attitude and allowed Him to open my eyes to the truth!

That was when He sent us to the Navajo Nation, to a people even more damaged than the Russians. That was when He shifted me from being a missionary to my real calling as an intercessor! This was a calling that would set me on a course that would forever change my life.

Intercessor

I've actually always been an intercessor. I just didn't know it. Yea, I *acted* like a missionary and thought that was my calling for a number of years, but all that time, I was really an intercessor. At this point you might ask, "How did you know"? Answer: I didn't! That's why I thought I was a missionary! Are you confused yet? I certainly was!

Something I have known for quite some time is that we serve a multifaceted God who is not moved by our limited understanding of either who we are or who we think He is. He is the "I Am that I Am"! He is the same yesterday, today, and forever (Hebrews 13:8). The problem, as I see it, is that we limit ourselves by our finite understanding of who we think we are and what we think God wants to do through us. I believe that God knows His Word a whole lot better than we do! I also believe that many Christians limit what God does in and through them because of their limited understanding of His will and Word.

As I mentioned before, I've always been a "hear and obey" person. For me, the best time of the day is when I get alone with God, lost in worship, lost in

His Presence, praying for whatever or whoever comes to mind. I can't really remember when I transitioned from just praying for my needs and the needs of those around me to praying according to His leading, but I did know that as I prayed, thoughts would flow through my mind that I could not have possibly come up with on my own. I would pray out those thoughts until I felt a release or a peace about the situation. Usually I would pray scriptures—lots of them! If it's in His Word, it's in His will!

I would start out worshipping Him and just inviting His Holy Spirit to come. Then sometimes I would have thoughts that I knew were from Him or I would see a picture in my mind's eye and begin to pray about it. As I prayed, it was like He took over and prayed through me. Sometimes there would be groaning and intense emotion. Sometimes there would be a militant attitude as He rebuked demons and declared His will and purpose for a situation. I wouldn't quit praying until I ran out of words. I would sense that we were done. Let me be very succinct on this: It was not my doing, but His. I was simply a yielded vessel for what He wanted done. I was and am no one special. I am a vessel of His choosing for the purpose of prayer and intercession. It was always about Him, His will, and desires for this earth.

I used to think that everyone prayed that way, at least those who were actively serving the Lord. Jesus taught a lot about prayer in His Word, and it was my understanding that everyone who really wanted to serve the Lord would spend time in prayer and worship, study

His Word, and witness to the lost. Fundamentally, this is all true; however, there is a difference between many people's daily prayer time and the labor of intercession.

I used to mentally beat myself up all time over the issue of evangelism. Sure, there were occasions that I was able to share the Gospel with someone who didn't know Jesus yet, and I even got to pray with some, but these times were few and far between. I used to wonder what was wrong with me. Often I would be in a conversation with someone, and it wouldn't even occur to me to ask if they knew the Lord or not. Sometimes I knew they didn't, but I could not seem to find the right words to say to them to show how concerned I was for their soul. Then I would be with another Christian who seemed to share their faith with everyone with the ease of simply asking the time. Why was this so hard for me?

Conversely, others would hear me pray during corporate prayer times and stare at me with open mouths. Often people would come up to me privately asking for prayer stating that they knew if I said I would pray for their situation that I really would pray! They were right! I could not turn down a sincere prayer request. Sometimes, God would tell me things about these situations that went deeper than the request. This was usually the root issue why prayer had previously been ineffective. I would share with the appropriate person what God had told me. Sometimes it would be a lightbulb moment and the situation would shift. Sometimes they would deny the problem and go on their way. I was just trying to obey God in all things.

As I began to ask God about what was really going on, He began to teach me about callings and giftings. Just because the church put women ministers in a box did not mean that God wanted us there! He explained that most people pray their needs and what's on their hearts, but His intercessors were a handpicked team of warriors willing to go places in prayer and do things that never even crossed most people's minds. We are a strategic part of His plan in the earth. We are called. Just like all are called to win the lost, but evangelists are specially gifted to *really* win the lost! All are called to pray, but not all are called to war, contend, pray prophetically, and take back ground from the enemy on a routine basis. We all may have opportunities to teach biblical truths to our fellow believers, but not all spend hours in research to teach the body of Christ. I think you get the picture.

This was awesome! I could lay down the guilt trip about evangelism and help others lay down their guilt trip about prayer! I still won someone to the Lord occasionally, taught a little, worked in the nursery or food pantry, but I was now free to serve the Lord in a way that delighted both Him and me! I began to study about strategic kinds of prayer: what worked and what didn't. I read books about dealing with the demonic and spiritual mapping. (See appendix A for a list of my favorite books.) In the beginning, there not much out there to read, but as time went on, lots of books popped up everywhere! I also did a lot of biblical studies on my own.

By the time we moved to the Navajo Nation, I understood that demons were not everywhere, but they did inhabit certain places where they had been invited in by previous events or persons. One of the main giftings I noticed among intercessors is the discerning of spirits. In some places I would notice that the atmosphere felt "clean." In other places, there would be a heavy or oppressive feeling. I knew demons were present. These were usually places where innocent blood was shed, evil was perpetrated, or false gods (demons) were worshiped. In places that were infested by demons, people's eyes were blinded to the truth making ministry of any kind very difficult!

When we moved to the Navajo Nation, almost everywhere we went felt oppressive! Idol worship was rife in the area as was drunkenness, abuse, and unemployment. The Navajo didn't care for white people and weren't interested in the white man's religion. I went to the library to do some research about the area. What I discovered was appalling!

In the mid-1800s, the army established Fort Defiance, in "defiance" of the Navajo people (or Dine as they called themselves). There were many raids, broken treaties, the stealing and slaughter of livestock, and even selling of some Navajo captives into slavery. It all culminated into what the Navajo refer to as "The Long Walk" where they were forcibly relocated from their homes to Fort Sumner, New Mexico about 450 miles away[9]. The army burned their crops and herded them into Canyon De Chelly where they rounded them up and forced them to walk the whole way. Many of the very young and very old died. The "relocation" was a miserable failure, and the Navajo were allowed to return to their own land about four and a half years later.

After they returned, some of the prominent Christian denominations at that time sent missionaries to the Navajo. The expenses of some of these missionaries were paid by the federal government in exchange for some "spying" on the Navajo people on behalf of the government! Additionally, the missionaries made converts cut their hair and dress like the white people. Children in the schools had to speak English and were not permitted to speak their native tongue under threat of punishment. No wonder the Navajo disliked the whites and wanted nothing to do with their religion! Missions efforts have been a struggle in the area ever since.

We did do some missions work, helped with church camps and outreaches while we lived there. My husband had horses and used them to do trail rides and camping trips for the youth. We had some success with this but not much especially among the unchurched. Mostly I just prayed.

I prayed over maps, declaring what I felt the Lord wanted for different areas. I fasted, did all-night prayer meetings, whatever the Lord wanted to do. Then I met a lady who was organizing a re-creation of the Long Walk. Each church or group was assigned a ten-mile segment to walk and pray on a specified day. We were able to organize two groups from two different churches for the twenty miles between Sawmill and Window Rock. The day arrived. The weather had been pretty nice before this, but on the very day, it snowed—hard! We figured the devil didn't want us to do this, so we did it anyway! Then we met in the middle at Fort Defiance at the only remaining building from the original 1860s fort. We were a mixed group of whites and Navajos. We prayed and then some of the whites asked the Navajo to forgive them for the atrocities of their ancestors. Something shifted in the heavenlies; we felt it!

Not much outwardly changed, but we knew we had accomplished what the Lord wanted us to do. Intercession is often like that. The intercessor sees what God wants things to look like, hears what He wants to do, and prays it into place. Sometimes the Lord has us walk or drive an area while praying over it. Sometimes we fast according to His leading. Sometimes we pray in the night watches because strategic things happen at strategic times[10]. Sometimes the Lord will have us do something symbolic and/or bring forth decrees into the atmosphere of a place.

If this all seems kind of weird to you, remember that Elisha had men put salt into a new jar to heal the waters of Jericho (2 Kings 2:19–22). Jesus spit on the ground, made a mud pack, and placed it on a man's eyes to heal them (John 9:6–7). The Bible is full of such varied and "weird" examples: symbolic acts to break through demonic barriers, bringing healing and deliverance.

Often, we never see the far-reaching effects of the intercession we do. When a building is built, it takes a long time to prepare the ground, lay the plumbing and electric, and build the foundation. It seems like the building project is taking forever, taking a lot of money and effort, yet still no completed building. Subcontractors come in and do their parts, but still the building isn't completed. It takes a lot of time, money, and effort to see the completed work. Intercession is much the same way. Some intercessors will come in and break up the ground, another will lay the foundation. By the time breakthrough takes place resulting in evangelism, salvations, healings, and deliverances, and even to city-wide or regional transformation, whole teams of intercessors over years and decades have come and gone. Each contributed their part. Without them, the work would not have been completed.

We moved every three to six years. Back in the "I thought I was a missionary" days, I really struggled with all the moving. It seemed like we would go to an area, labor for breakthrough, do everything the Lord asked of us, and just when things were beginning to turn around, He would move us to another place to start all over again. I was getting frustrated. Others were partaking of the fruits of our labors, but we did not even get a taste! I wanted to put roots down, make some friends, and shift from all the labor-intensive warfare and intercession to training the new believers. It was never to be.

I asked the Lord about it one day. I was tired of moving, new locations, new churches, new acquaintances, new jobs. He said something very interesting that I will never forget. "You and your husband are burden bearers. Like Aaron and Hur, you go to places where my servant needs his arms held up because he no longer has strength for the battle. You are a frontline warrior; part of My special forces. You go to places that no one else will go to and contend with demonic forces that others are afraid of to bring My Kingdom into the earth. You are a groundbreaker.

You lay a foundation that others can build on. I have very few servants who are willing to pack up and move on My orders and start all over again, but you were raised military and understand that I must relocate forces to strategic places on the front lines in order to win the battle."

We've been criticized by church members for what we do. We've lost friends over the years, never been able to buy a house and settle down. I've never worked at a job long enough to earn any decent retirement, but I would not trade all the things of this world for what the Lord has done in my life. If I had it to do over again, I would not make the same mistakes I did, but I would still follow Him to the ends of the earth! Little did I know how hard the next level of intercession would be. Little did I know how hot the battle would really become.

The Vision and the Dreams

The year 2006 was a pivotal year for me. At face value, it didn't look any different, and it started the same as any other year. I was working, worshiping, praying, studying God's Word, and interceding for the people and church that I was assigned to by the Lord. I'm not really sure what precipitated the shift, but the shift did indeed take place.

I didn't know we were about to change locations again, didn't know we would enter a whole new level of warfare, and I especially didn't know that instead of victory, the enemy was about to win yet another battle. I also had no clue that the Lord was about to open up to me a whole new area of prophetic dreams and revelation!

It really started in what we Westerners call the month of August. It was the first day of Elul on the Hebrew calendar. I didn't at that time understand the significance, but God knew exactly what He was up to!

Elul begins a season known to the Jewish people as the forty days of teshuvah. It is the period of time leading up to the fall feast days of Rosh Hashanah (Feast of Trumpets), Yom Kippur (Day of Atonement), and Sukkoth (Feast of Tabernacles). It is a season of repentance, a time for God's people to turn their hearts back to Him.[11] "The thirty days of Elul are considered to be a time to reflect upon your destiny, a time to seek God concerning your spiritual future, and a time to obtain mercy."[12] The ten days between the Feast of Trumpets and the Day of Atonement are known as the "Days of Awe." It is believed that the heavens are opened during this period of time to hear the prayers and decrees of those who have repented.[13] When the heavens are opened, not only do our prayers get through without the usual warfare and hindrances but answers and revelation come back down to us (Genesis 28:12)!

As was my usual custom, I was up in the room the Lord had graciously provided me for prayer on that day, the first of Elul. I almost never get a vision; the Lord usually speaks to me by thoughts or impressions that I would not have come up with on my own. That day, I had a vision. I saw a map of the United States laid out before me. The old route 66 was in red and pulsing like an artery. The Lord said, "Redeem this for Me." My response was, "Who, me"? Like there was anyone *else* in the room at the time! Then I began to argue with the Lord: "I'm just a local intercessor. I don't have any connections to do this. Why don't you have someone like Cindy Jacobs do it?" God was not deterred or impressed by my logic. He said nothing in response to my questions. He simply repeated the command.

I didn't know what to do or where to begin, so I put it on the shelf. It then occurred to me that the last several years had been spent laboring in churches along route 66. Maybe God had been up to something for a while that I didn't fully understand?

Since we left Russia, victories had been few and far between. The Lord kept sending us to churches with pastors who said they wanted true revival, but after all the fasting, prayer, and intercessions, they were not willing to pay the price. In each instance, the local demonic strongman was uncovered, but that pastor was unwilling to do what was necessary to pull him down so that the Holy Spirit would be free to move. When it became obvious that nothing further would be accomplished in a particular location, the Lord would move us to the next duty station. I understood that moving didn't mean that the enemy had won and the local congregation would not get what they desired. It just meant that it wasn't time yet, and we were needed elsewhere. Sometimes people just have to go around that mountain again until they are ready to slay the giants!

I knew once again that we were changing duty stations, but I didn't know exactly when. The Lord did show me that if the contending was successful, He would raise up a place where wounded sheep would be healed, trained up, and sent out. He also gave me the number "500." Although at that time I didn't know what it would mean. When we arrived at the new duty station, the pastor there said, "I know what the 500 means! The Lord promised me 500 people if I would take back this church!" We were excited about what God was getting ready to do!

The Word the Lord gave me for the next duty station was "For thus the Lord GOD, the Holy One of Israel, has said, 'In repentance and rest you will be saved, In quietness and trust is your strength.'" (Isaiah 30:15, NASB). If I had known we were in the season of repentance, it would have been my prayer focus. Isaiah 30:15 ends with "but you were not willing" (NASB). I didn't see any of it until it was too late.

The first day of Tishrei, Rosh Hashanah, the Feast of Trumpets, God gave me a dream. I was not in the habit of getting downloads in the night watches from the Lord, but all that was about to change. In the dream, I found myself ascending a broad flight of stairs. When I reached the top of the stairs, I found myself at a door to a restaurant. The sign on the door said, "No shirt, No shoes, No service." I looked down at my feet and saw that they were bare. I turned aside to go find some shoes. I knew that there was an important meeting about to take place in the restaurant that I was supposed to be in. I also knew that I needed plain, brown sandals, and then I would be allowed into the meeting. As I walked away from the restaurant, I discovered myself in a mall in front of a shoe store. I went inside, but all they had was various colored dress shoes and high heels. I went into another store, but they had colored beach sandals and flip-flops. I was not able to find any plain brown sandals. Then I woke up. When I took this to prayer, the Lord did not interpret the dream for me, but He did say that the dream and the vision were related.

I began to look for the answers. I needed to know what the interpretation was and how the two were related. I needed to know what my part in all this was supposed to be. I wrote to several prominent ministries that I knew operated in the prophetic, but I didn't get an answer from anyone. I searched out books on dream interpretation and prayed more, but no answers were forthcoming.

In the meantime, decisions were made, things came together, and we moved to our next duty station. This would prove to be a strategic move for us in more ways than one. Historically, I would pray with people at my local church but had just started connecting with regional intercessors for prayer. The new state that we moved to had an established group of intercessors that were organized, connected, and supportive of one another! I would get to be part of a team of people of like mind who understood where I was coming from and, more importantly, were as passionate about the Lord as I was!

I submitted the dream and the vision to the leader of that team. She responded and said that brown denotes warmth, the color of the earth, and that shoes denoted favor. Ascending stairs usually means going to another level. Well, it certainly made sense to me that I didn't have the necessary favor or credentials to attend a gathering for the redemption of a major artery of our nation. By this time, I knew that route 66 was entrenched in independence and rebellion; it was all about the "me" generation. I knew it would have to be a group effort and somehow I would have to find favor.

I didn't have favor, didn't have a strategic battle plan from the Lord, didn't even know if I was ready to ascend to another level, and didn't know the timing for this endeavor! Since I didn't know as much as I did know, I decided to wait on the Lord to see what He would open up and when. It seemed to me that the Lord was not interested in a prayer drive or the usual strategically placed prayer meetings that we had done in the past. I wondered if He wanted to do something new, but I didn't know what it was. I sensed this was big—was important to Him—and I didn't want to screw it up!

Waiting was not my strong suit, but I had no choice. Wait is what I did. Life went on; I went to work, went to church, fasted and prayed according to the Lord's leading, studied His Word. Time seemed to drag on. My prayer focus shifted from the national level to the local again. Not that I didn't pray nationally, but I spent much more time in prayer for the local church and area that I was directly involved with.

The Lord called me to a twenty-one-day fast for the area. I was new here and didn't have much background information, but I had learned to fast and pray according to His leading, so I was not too concerned. Whatever God wanted to get done, He would do.

On the third day of the fast, a little boy in our area was abducted from his bus stop. I added his plight to the list of things I was seeking from the Lord. A few days later, I felt impressed by God to declare that the police would be sovereignly directed to the place where he was being held and that he would be found safe. Later that same day, the police went to serve a warrant at an apartment complex and noted a vehicle of interest in the parking lot. They found the apartment belonging to the vehicle and discovered not only the recently abducted boy, but also another boy who had been missing for four years!

I don't believe for a minute that my prayers were what brought the boys back to safety. After all, I didn't know anything about the other boy and had never prayed for him. I do believe that many people had been praying for four long years for the other boy and the bowls of intercession were almost full. When the second boy disappeared, fresh cries of intercession went up to heaven, the bowls overflowed, and God declared what He wanted to happen in order to return both boys back home.

Prayer warfare involves victories and defeats, gains and losses, hindrances and breakthroughs, revelation and misunderstanding. I still didn't know that I was in a major shift; that God was opening up to me a whole new realm of dreams. Nor did I understand that I would need to learn to correctly interpret these dreams *and the timing* in order to stay in step with what God wanted to do. If only I knew then what I know now.

What I did know was that per diem nursing has a different interpretation from state to state. In one state, it means you can work as much as you want. In another state it means that you can get cut from the schedule as much as they want. I was in the latter.

One morning in April, I awoke early since I was scheduled to work. I really needed to work since I had been cut so much already and was concerned about the reduced pay. They always call to cancel two hours before the start of the shift because if they don't and you come in to work, they have to pay you for two hours.

This particular morning, I had a strange dream that I didn't remember initially, but the dream came back to me in prayer. Unfortunately, I didn't have time to wait on the Lord for the interpretation and pray through it and get to work on time. I felt impressed to call work to see if they needed me but figured that two hours pay was better than nothing. I thought I would have time to pray later. I was wrong. I went to work, found out I was indeed cancelled, and returned home. As I was driving home, I heard something on the news that brought tears to my eyes. Then I knew what the dream meant.

In the dream I was walking down a dirt road. It was deer season. All along the side of the road there were deer, lots of them, both male and female. Some were sitting, some lying down, some were standing. All of them were wounded and bleeding. Some of them had arrows sticking out of their sides. Many were mortally wounded. None of them moved as I walked down the road. They watched me go by, pleading with their eyes for me to do something for them. I was bewildered. Then I woke up.

On the news that day, a gunman had opened fire at a college killing thirty-two people and wounding seventeen others in two separate attacks over a two-hour period of time. I don't know why God used deer to portray college students, but I do know that if I had stayed home and prayed, He would have given me the intercessory burden necessary for the interpretation. I went to work at about the time of the first attacks. By the time I returned home, it was over.

I will always wonder if I could have stopped or at least lessened the severity of the attacks in prayer. I don't know if God had called on several intercessors that day and no one responded or not enough of us did. Perhaps nothing could have changed the outcome, and God was simply trying to teach me something. I'll never know the answers to these questions this side of heaven. What I do know is that this was not God's doing. It was the devil working through a chosen agent to perpetrate evil. I also know that I will never ignore a dream or a call to prayer again!

Another thing I learned was that God often shares dreams with us in the night watches, but we discard them as "pizza" dreams, think we will remember them later and pray over them then, or can't imagine that God would actually give us a dream of any significance. After all, we are only just created in His image, fearfully and wonderfully made, and the hairs on our head numbered! Who are we to think that God would actually want to give us a dream!? (I'm being sarcastic here.) I have to admit that I've had my sleep disturbed by demonic dreams, had a lot of "process dreams" (the brain working out the stuff of the day), and had some God-inspired dreams. I just simply don't want to miss what God is saying.

Over the course of the next few years, the Lord gave me many dreams, words of knowledge and revelation. Most of these had to do with local people or places and were for the immediate time frame or near future. One thing I did learn was that the more time I spent with Him, the more things He shared with me. My personal opinion is that God is always talking, always wanting to share secrets with His beloveds, but most of us most of the time don't spend enough time with Him.

We also don't often get all the information we would like to have concerning situations. Did we pray right? Did it work? One morning I had a dream of three fighter jets. One of them was in trouble and crashed to the earth tail down. I saw flames and ran over to the crash site. The pilot was still strapped in his seat but away from the flames. The pilot was moving and groaning. People were standing around, but doing nothing. I had someone call 911 and started to pray. As I prayed, the pilot came to and started to sing a hymn. I sang with him until emergency crews arrived. After I woke up, I immediately went to prayer for all our pilots in Iraq and Afghanistan. I don't know if any of them were in trouble, or about to be in trouble, but I was not going to miss my duty station! Who knows, maybe when I get to heaven I'll find out I helped save a life! I would like that very much.

So what of route 66? Would it surprise you to know that I still don't have all the answers and still haven't had a breakthrough after fifteen years of prayer and intercession for the area? I simply did what the Lord led me to do. I don't live and work on route 66 anymore, but I trust the Lord that all the labor that went into it was not in vain. He is not finished with it yet! Joseph waited twenty-two years for his dream to be fulfilled (Genesis 43:26). Moses waited forty years on the back side of the desert before the Lord called him forth! After what would subsequently happen to me there, I hope to never have to return; but if the Lord should ask me to do anything else concerning route 66, I will do it. Otherwise, I will wait to see what He does with what we have contended for. Others still labor there, and if they don't give up and don't give in to the devil, they will obtain the promise!

The Next Season and a New Level

People often prophesy about ascending to new levels, but I'm not convinced *they* know what they are talking about, let alone the ones they are prophesying to. I've been prophesied to quite a bit over the years. Usually, if the prophecy touches my heart, speaks to me in a way that I know it is from the Lord, I write it down. If it doesn't "do anything" for me, I discard it. The funny thing about prophecy is that if it is a Word from the Lord through another, or through a dream, even if it doesn't "do it" for me, God does not let me forget it.

The first time I remember being prophesied to was in the late 1970s. I was in a women's Bible study group and one of the women came up to me and gave me Psalm 91. I read it, and at the time it was meaningless. Little did I know that as a warrior intercessor, Psalm 91 would become very special to me! Often in prayer battles, I would quote various parts of it so the devil would know I meant business and I was protected! God was my refuge and fortress, my deliverer (Psalm 91:2)! No evil would be able to come near me (Psalm 91:10).

I've known for a long time that in order to be able to claim and declare the promises of God, you have to meet the conditions. Ps 91:1 is the condition. I strived to remain in His shelter and under His shadow. I knew I could not claim the protections listed in the Psalm unless I met the condition of verse one. It was kind of tricky. I thought I was covered, firmly in His shelter, but there were some things I didn't know that allowed me to be shifted out from under that shelter. It was subtle and deceptive taking me completely by surprise, but more of that later.

The year 2008 became the year of the next season and a new level. I usually start off the year by joining Jentezen Franklin's church in their twenty-one-day January fast. It gives me an opportunity to set the tone for the year to come and see what the Lord is saying about that particular year. I don't recall if I heard anything significant that January, but I sure didn't write anything down in my prayer journal!

I did, however, start having more prophetic dreams that year that increased over the course of the next few years. At first I was a little concerned about the dreams because the Word says, "Your young men will see visions, your old men will dream dreams" (Acts 2:17b, cjb). Yea, so I am a grandma, but I certainly didn't feel old! I could almost hear the Lord laughing at that one! I did ask Him about it, and He had a very interesting observation. He told me that dreams require a level of maturity to correctly interpret and that many of His young believers simply would not know how to interpret them. That certainly made me feel better!

Little did I know at that time that I didn't possess the level of maturity necessary to interpret them either!

The first significant dream I had that year was of the Lord. In the dream, I was walking down a path to a house. A man with shoulder-length wavy hair joined me on the path. His countenance was haggard. He wore a robe common to first-century men. I knew he was a king. He carried a scepter and a crown on a red velvet pillow. He didn't say anything but handed me the crown on the pillow to carry for him. As we walked into the house, I noticed that it appeared run-down and unkempt. We walked into the front room where I noticed a few overweight people laying on couches and recliners. They were snacking on what appeared to be chips and junk food. They looked at us but didn't bother to get up or say anything. There was more of the same in the other rooms of the house. The king walked back into the main room after inspecting the other rooms and lifted his scepter up. When he did, the house began to fill with aqua-blue clear water. He led me out of the house and instructed everyone to climb trees to avoid the flood. The house began to bulge with the water, then it burst. The water leveled the house and flooded the surrounding area. Many people were up in the trees, but none of those in the house made it out.

I struggled with the interpretation. I prayed over it but didn't get a whole lot except that the house denoted the church. The people in it were lazy, overfed, and apathetic. The King is coming to see the condition of His house. It needed cleansing. I didn't know if it was about a specific church or a type of church or denomination. I prayed that the people of God would wake up, understand the age we live in, and that they each had a destiny to fulfill. We are part of a vast army in a heavenly kingdom, not spectators at a movie or sports arena. I believe that the church is in need of cleansing. I also understood that for those of us in tune with His voice, we may be asked to do some unusual things to escape cleansing judgments. It is not up to us to question Him. It is up to us to obey.

Each year has a biblical and numerical significance. Chuck Pierce taught about the year 2008 in his Issachar school course on "Interpreting the Times." He taught that it would be a year of new beginnings, a year of completion turning into fullness, a year of travail turning into birth. It would also be a year of finding new entrances and watching all gates, a year of revelation. There was also this thing about warring generationally for your inheritance, a year of circumcision, and making sure the enemy didn't get into the gates.[14]

I knew about the new beginnings and travail turning into birth, but I hadn't yet put the rest of it together. I was very excited about finally being able to be part of the birth that I had labored so hard for after all these years of pursuing the Lord and His presence. This just *had* to be the year! I knew I needed to go to another level in the Lord. After all, if we are going to have true revival that's sustainable over the long run, we would have to look like and act like the early church. We were not there. Where were the healings and miracles? Where were all the salvations, the tears of repentance?

That summer I decided to pursue the Lord fully and ask Him for a deeper relationship in Him, a new level. He granted my request and the dreams increased. I also was tired of battling frustration. I loved my husband, but he simply didn't seem interested in pursuing the Lord like I wanted to. It seemed like instead of us being partners in the Lord's work, I was dragging him along with me. The enemy had me convinced that my husband was holding me back and that I didn't really need him to be involved in the work I was doing. I didn't know, of course, that this mind-set was part of the enemy's diabolical scheme to undermine the Lord's work. I thought it was just me. I thought that I was protecting my husband by keeping him out of the spiritual battles I was involved in. I didn't understand that the Lord had strategically placed my husband in my life to cover and protect me in my intercessory prayer work and that I needed to tell him everything I was involved in so he could do just that. I would later learn one of the hardest lessons of my entire life. Covering is critical!

The week prior to the dream about the run-down house and the king, I had another dream. At the time it made no sense to me but would turn out to be strategically significant. In the dream I saw blue contact lenses in a stack in a small lens case. My husband brought them home and asked me to get him a pair (my husband has worn contacts for most of his life and has blue eyes). I opened the case not knowing there were several pairs in there and spilled them in the sink. I didn't lose any of them but got them mixed up. At that time, the interpretation the Lord gave me was that my husband is to pick out his own lenses. He is the only one who knows how to handle them. I should have known that my husband could "see" things I couldn't see, but I didn't understand, and within three years' time, hell would have its way.

An interesting thing happened in 2009. I had registered for Chuck Pierce's annual "Starting Your Year Off Right" conference, but my very elderly father-in-law was dying. We didn't know how much time he would have, and I know this sounds kind of selfish, but it would be very inconvenient of him to go home during the conference! We lived about eight hours away and would have to leave immediately if we got a call from one of the nurses taking care of him. I simply asked the Lord if He could wait to take my father-in-law home until the conference was over. He did. As soon as the conference was completed, that very day, we got the phone call. After we arrived, one of the nurses said something very interesting. She said that a few nights ago Dad was "hallucinating." He was looking up at the ceiling and said, "If you want me to wait a few more days, I can do that." I believe he was talking to the Lord and gave the Lord permission to answer my prayer! Wow, what a God we serve!

One of the emphases of that conference was that there is a visitation of the Lord coming that would facilitate a great harvest of souls with signs, wonders, and miracles. This would have to be contended for. Holiness is the gate. The Lord spoke to me to shift my intercession from hedges of protection to holiness and purity. He said that this is how we would take the enemy in the gate.

The year 2009 became not only the year of increased prayer warfare, but increased prophetic dreams and revelation. I had asked the Lord for this, but now that He had granted my request, I didn't know what to do with it all. Neither did anyone else in my immediate circle. I brought much of this information to my pastor thinking he would help me walk through it, but it was beyond him as well.

The next dream I had I managed to totally screw up and misinterpret! In this dream I was standing alone on a beach with my compound hunting bow and a full quiver of arrows. I saw many enemies come up out of the sea, so I began shooting at them. In the next scene, I found myself in a house filled with food. There was food everywhere: spilling out of cupboards, on countertops, and stacked high on the tables. I laid my bow down and wondered at all the food. Then I turned and there was one of the enemy standing at the door. He was small in stature and held an antique bow in his hand. He had one field-tipped arrow (these are used for practice, not hunting) pointed at me. He demanded my pocket knife. I gave him the knife. Suddenly, arrows were being shot at him from somewhere outside the house. He released the arrow he had pointed at me, then threw my knife back at me, and fled. The arrow hit me in a rib but didn't penetrate very deep. I was able to easily pull it out. I ducked as he threw the knife, and it lodged in the door jam. Then my husband showed up leading the attack against the enemy. He saw that I was wounded and insisted I go to the hospital, but when we went, there were delays and confusion. I didn't receive any treatment. We then went to report the incident to the police, but again confusion reigned. I woke up.

The sea almost always denotes a group of people or the world. The enemies are demons. People are not the enemy. They can be used by the enemy, but they are not the enemy. I believed at that time (and still do) that the house denotes the church. It is full of bread (teaching). There is so much teaching in the church that many take it for granted and do not even partake of it anymore. In the dream, I was standing alone ready to defend the church against the enemy. I had forgotten that the year before, the Lord told me to wait for reinforcements. Even then, I was doing okay for a while until I let my guard down. The demon that attacked me was small and used an ancient weapon (religion and tradition). The attack would have been totally ineffective if I hadn't let my guard down, but I felt safe in the church. The pocket knife was given to me by my father-in-law, and I knew at that time that it signified my inheritance. I thought it was a financial inheritance, but it would turn out to be my spiritual inheritance, my destiny that the enemy would try to steal.

I knew this was a warning dream, but I never figured it out until after the fact. I spent the next year trying to figure out practically what this attack would look like and how to prevent it. Instead, I ran headlong right smack into the middle of it and never saw it coming! I was trying to protect a physical inheritance and keep my husband from leading me into confusion when in fact I needed my husband to cover and protect me. I thought a literal demon would come to steal a physical inheritance, but instead, the enemy used a close friend to try to remove me from my destiny and calling. My husband would be the one to come to the rescue!

The next dream I had I was walking into a naval shipyard. There were several old rusty ships moored there. I saw a man with a welding torch working on one of these ships. He was removing scrap metal and laying it in a pile. I asked him what he was doing, and he said, "I can't just leave these ships to rot away. I have to try to clean them up and refit them for service or turn them into scrap metal." After I woke up, I asked the Lord about the dream. He said, "That's how many of My people are. They are not in service anymore, rotting away. If they will submit to My cleansing and refurbishing, I can still use them in My work."

The cleansing process can be very painful, but our Lord's heart cry was and still is for holiness, righteousness, and purity. He wants us to be fit and looking good, not rotting away somewhere in the junk pile of life. We each have a purpose, a destiny. No matter how old we are, we have to find His purpose for our lives. Otherwise, we will never be truly happy or complete.

The Lord gave me many dreams that year. Most had to do with local and immediate situations, but some would turn out to be significant years later. Some were of national rather than local importance. The Lord was teaching me to write them down immediately so I would not forget the details and submit them to Him in prayer for the interpretation. As time went on, I began to realize that He was not going to give me the whole interpretation immediately. Sometimes I would have to wait as bits and pieces came together. I also had to be very careful not to try to figure everything out for myself! I learned the hard way that a misinterpreted dream can wreak havoc!

The next significant dream the Lord gave me that year was about a hippo! In the dream I saw a large hippo in a house (here we are back in church again). It acted like it belonged, like it owned the place. It went into the backyard where there was a swimming pool. The hippo demanded that the pool be drained of the clear, chlorinated water and be replaced with regular water. Then it went into the pool and demanded to be fed. It dirtied up the water. As long as the people in the house fed and cared for it and left the water dirty, it stayed submerged in the pool. You could look at the pool and not even know it was in there. It only came up to be fed again. The pastor was in the house watching the people feed the hippo.

I looked up everything I could find out on the Internet about hippos, but nothing was making sense. I knew there was a spirit that was fouling up the church and making demands but didn't know how to get rid of it. The pastor didn't know what to do about it either. I later discovered that biblically, behemoth is translated as hippo. Job 40:19b says that behemoth is the first of God's strength and "only his maker can approach him with his sword" (CJB). Job 40:24 states, "Can anyone capture him when he is on watch, With barbs can anyone pierce his nose?" (NASB).

This was not just some petty spirit that we could easily dislodge. We needed God's strategic battle plan. The church people were feeding it—*that* was not going to make it any easier. I sought God for a battle plan, but nothing came to mind. I've never been one to back down from a fight. I always assumed that if God revealed demons, it was for the purpose of dealing with them. After all, "Greater is He who is in you than he who is in the world" (1 John 4:4b, NASB). It never occurred to me that maybe the church didn't want me messing with their hippo! Maybe that's why instead of doing the obvious, Jesus would ask people what they wanted Him to do for them. Sometimes we just have to know when to stand and fight and when to walk away. There was soon coming a time when I stood and fought by myself when I should have walked away.

I had many dreams that year about birthing and the enemy trying to steal the baby or about being in revival and someone coming in to take it over. Each time, I would intercede about the situation. We needed the manifest presence of God. I desperately wanted Him and assumed that everyone else in the church did too. It never occurred to me that maybe they were happy with their denominational mind-set, happy to feed the hippo. God can come and give us warm fuzzies, heal our bodies, help us financially and with our families, but clean us up? Ask us to stop feeding the hippo? It was not to be. That was asking too much.

I struggled that year with praying for holiness and praying for protection for everyone. I hated to see people get hurt. I just wanted everyone to come alongside of the Lord's plan, do what He wanted them to do, and be who He wanted them to be. I've never been a fire and brimstone, turn or burn kind of person, and God wasn't asking me to pick up an old methodology, but He is still the same yesterday, today, and forever. Holiness and repentance was the order of the day, and His church wasn't getting it.

The next dream I had was a different variation on the same theme. In the dream, my husband and I were trying to get our new RV down a narrow road. We got stopped at a bridge. Someone had left several pieces of old equipment on the bridge blocking our way. I got out to see what could be done when a man came up to me and dropped a dead body on the bridge facedown in front of me. He appeared to have been in his thirties and had obviously been dead for several days. A heated discussion ensued on how to get the body off the bridge so we could get through, but the man who had brought the body wanted him officially declared dead by a medical doctor. I argued that it was obvious he was dead, and we didn't need a doctor. I also noticed people lining the bank of the river that the bridge went over. They had fishing poles but were not catching anything.

In many of the denominational churches I had been in, there were plenty of middle-aged and older people but not very many young adults. It was apparent to me from this dream that the flow of the new that God wanted to bring forth was being blocked. We were losing the youth and young adults. Some church members were "standing by" to catch these as they floated along, but instead these young people were drowning in the river of this world.

My husband and I had lived our whole lives in houses. We had accumulated a lot of stuff over the years. When we moved into the RV, we had to get rid of all the old stuff, the old baggage. No matter how much we liked that stuff, there wasn't room for it, and it had to go. We had to get rid of a lot of appliances and all the old furniture and buy newer, more compact versions. The old equipment had to go if we were going to be able to live in the new!

That year some of the older people in our church passed on to glory, but I don't believe that is what the Lord was referring to. He was planning to take them home anyway. I believe He wanted us to get rid of old religious mind-sets. Adopt a new name; bury some of the old traditions. It was simply too much for them to handle.

I've never been known to give up without a fight. The year 2010 saw an increase in prayer and fasting and a dramatic increase in the dreams. The presence of the Lord during my prayer times was deeper and richer than it had ever been in my life. It seemed, however, that no matter how hard I prayed and interceded, we were not making much headway. Something was wrong, but I couldn't put my finger on it, at least not right then.

Acceleration to Nowhere

"Damn the torpedoes, full speed ahead!" This was quoted by Admiral David Farragut when he commanded the fleet entering Mobil Bay, Alabama, in 1864. His lead armored ship, the Tecumseh, was destroyed by a tethered mine (referred to as torpedoes in those days). As he uttered those famous words, "He swung his own ship clear and headed across the mines, which failed to explode. The fleet followed and anchored above the forts, which, now isolated, surrendered one by one."[15]

Of all the naval sayings I grew up hearing, this one describes me the best! The problem with mines is that sometimes they explode! Sometimes you can go through them "full speed ahead," but most of the time, you have to navigate mine fields painstakingly slow. The Lord is, more often than not, into "painstakingly slow"!

The year 2010 began the decade on the Hebrew calendar of the 5770s or the "Iyan" decade. This Hebrew letter signifies the eye, so we can say that the eye of the Lord is upon us. He is watching over us and also watching us to see how we'll respond to situations and circumstances. The devil also has an eye. He "stalks

about like a roaring lion looking for someone to devour"
(1 Peter 5:8b, CJB).

In January of 2010, Chuck Pierce brought forth an
interesting prophecy. He said:

> I am putting something together in you and for
> you that is very unique. I am recreating what
> you tried to create. *You have longed to finalize
> things but now you will see that you cannot put
> together your own puzzle.* You've even tried
> to put together other people around you and
> their puzzle. However, over that which I have
> created for them, I am holding the missing
> piece. This has frustrated you. You kept looking
> for the other piece and looking for the piece
> for someone else, but now you realize that it
> was you that I was dealing with. And *now*, I
> am going to show you the missing piece—your
> piece! I have sent signs in the heavens to let you
> know that only I am in control of time. Know
> this—I am determined to complete the project
> in you that I began. Wait for the placement.
> Wait for your placement![16]

I've always said that "wait" is a four-letter word!
I could not begin to imagine how different was the
puzzle of my life that God was putting together for
me. Nor could I imagine that my placement would be
anywhere else than the places I had contended for. I
don't know why I would think that way. Most soldiers
don't settle down in the place of the battle. They give it
back to whom it was intended for and return to their

own place. The only problem was I didn't have "my own place"!

If I had paid any real attention to the dreams and prophecies that were coming forth at that time in my life, I would have detected a totally different flow. I was in warfare contending mode. "Damn the torpedoes, full speed ahead!" I reasoned that with enough prayer and fasting, nothing would be impossible, nothing would be withheld! We would get the revival everyone said they wanted. Souls would be saved. People would be delivered and healed. Life would be good! God was trying to tell me something else. Of course, He wanted salvations, healings, and deliverances, but it all had to come together His way in His time. I was not interested in waiting.

Usually what the Lord reveals to me during the January prayer and fasting of each year sets the tone and the flow for that year. He gave me another dream. In this dream, I was at a Perry Stone conference. I had a large stack of books I wanted to purchase and went to the registers to pay for them. The first two were busy, but no one was at the third register. Perry came up to the register to ring up my purchase. I told him how much I appreciated his teaching. He thanked me and acted like he wished to speak with me further, but he didn't say anything. I then turned to go to the restroom but walked past it to the lodging area. I didn't believe I needed lodging and realized I had missed the restroom, so I turned to go back. I saw Perry sitting up on a balcony talking with some people. There was an empty seat where he was, and it seemed to me that I would be welcome to go up there, sit, and speak with him if I wanted to. He then looked at me, pointed toward the place I had come from, and said, "That is the best job here." I thought, "I don't need a job or lodging." I turned toward the restrooms and the sign on the door simply said, "Restroom," not ladies or women.

After I woke up, I tried to make some sense of the dream. Since the Lord didn't give me any immediate interpretation, I reasoned that to Perry the best job would be study of God's Word. I also decided that maybe I would finally get to "lodge" somewhere. Of course, in my mind, the somewhere ought to be where I already was!

Hindsight is *so* twenty-twenty! There is "a time for war and a time for peace" (Ecclesiastes 3:8). My heavenly Father was saying step back, study, slow down, enter my rest, lodge here for a while. I didn't "see" any of it. In April, during the counting of the Omer[17], the Lord showed me a picture of some stones. He said, "You have warred and contended, fasted and prayed for the breakthrough and have not yet laid hold of it. You have pressed in for an 'Elijah power encounter' thinking that will do it. It didn't work for Elijah and has become too heavy a burden for you. Step back and enter My rest. I will build *My* church, and the gates of hell will *not* prevail against it! Do not keep going to the church daily warring and contending. Give Me the stone of burden."

It was time for me to step back and receive fresh revelation. It was a time for increased study of His Word. It was a time to prepare and cleanse myself for the outpouring of His fire that would eventually come. However, I was a warrior, and all I really understood was warring and contending! I should have known, seen, and understood, but I didn't.

Neither did I remember that the scripture He first gave me for this particular duty station was "In repentance and rest you will be saved, In quietness and trust is your strength" (Isaiah 30:15, NASB). I had even written this in my prayer journal, but I forgot about it and didn't go back to reread it.

Instead, I pressed on toward the prize. I fasted and prayed. Nothing was breaking loose. What could be the hindrance? If "wait" was a four-letter word to me, then "give up" ran a close second. I figured if I warred, contended, fasted, and prayed enough we would finally get real revival!

In the meantime, a lot of prayer and fasting went up for a friend who was battling cancer and his wife for strength and endurance. I was convinced we would win this one. We also had a new grandbaby on the way that the enemy kept trying to deliver prematurely. I contended for her safe arrival. Little did I know that life as I knew it was already beginning to unravel.

I had another dream. In this dream I saw a man in an elaborate foreign uniform sitting on a horse. I understood that he was a leader of one of the European nations. As I watched him from behind, I saw a flash from a razor-thin sword come out of the sky. It severed his head from his body. A small trickle of blood went down his back, and then his head toppled from his body. Afterward, his body pitched forward off the horse. I marveled that there was so little blood. The sword had moved so fast that I did not actually see it cut his head off. I saw it move through the sky; then the guy's head fell off.

When I prayed about this dream, I felt that a change of government was coming suddenly to a nation unknown to me at that time. It would involve very little bloodshed. I was not to pray for this man's safety, but for a righteous leader to be raised up. The next day, I learned that the head of Poland had been killed in a plane crash. I would read in the news months later that the new leader was the very first president to invite the Israeli Prime Minister to Poland since the holocaust!

Why would God give me a dream about a nation that I had no connection to and had rarely prayed for? I don't have the answer to that. I suppose I was available and God needed a vessel to release prayer into the earth. I did believe because of the level of the presence of God in my life and the frequency of dreams He was giving me that I was right on track with what He wanted to do. I didn't realize at that time that my assumptions were not necessarily true. All it really meant was that I loved being with Him, and He liked spending time with me too! It didn't mean He was in full agreement with everything I was involved in!

I also worked with the regional intercessors prayer network for my location. At that time, we were just beginning to pray over all the local Masonic lodges. We had training by Dr. Bill Sudduth of Righteous Acts Ministries[18] on how to appropriately tear down the strongman of Freemasonry that has kept our nation bound. We participated in sessions of repentance and pulling out of generational bondages that might leave an open door to masonry in our own lives. We wanted to see these people set free and felt that we were trained and ready to do so! The training offered by this ministry was excellent in the areas of spiritual warfare and dealing with generational bondages. We went out in teams of intercessors—never alone.

We were about to enter the Hebrew year of 5771. It was the month of Av (Aug 10, 2010). The ninth of Av had come and gone without major difficulties, but later that month was another story! We were at the hospital anticipating the birth of our third grandchild. She had survived the enemy's attempt at miscarriage early in the pregnancy and the subsequent six weeks of preterm labor later on. Here we were laboring at the hospital for our granddaughter when a phone call came that I will never forget.

I usually enjoy getting phone calls from friends. It's a time to reconnect and enjoy fellowship with people far, far away that I might not get to see for a long time. Sometimes the phone can bring the worst of news. This was that kind of call. The friend that we had contended so hard for to be healed of cancer had taken a turn for the worse and was dying. I couldn't believe what I was hearing! I was assisting in the birth of my grandchild. The timing could not have been worse. Then things went from bad to worse. Our friend passed away, and then our grandbaby was born but wasn't breathing! The nurses worked frantically on her to get her to breathe, but she just wasn't responding and I couldn't even pray!

She was rushed off to the NICU, and I just stood there in shock. All I could do was cry, "Jesus!"

I was devastated. Our granddaughter turned out to be fine, but my best friend was grieving the loss of her husband. It was bittersweet to say the least! I did find it interesting though that my granddaughter who was born on 8-10, weighed in at 8 pounds, 10 ounces! I felt like maybe God was trying to tell us something, but I was too battle-weary to care. I wish I had known that the enemy was just getting started. I wish I knew how to avert the disaster!

Transition

The year of transition for me actually began on the ninth of Av, 5770, on the Jewish calendar (2010 on the Gregorian calendar). As was mentioned in the previous chapter, I had thought that the Jewish people had escaped tragedy that year, but mine was just beginning. I had just lost a friend and almost lost my granddaughter. The year from hell was just getting started!

The number eleven, interestingly enough, means transition! Transition, in and of itself, can be either good or bad. When I think of transition, I think about that stage of the labor process where the cervix is finally fully dilated allowing the baby to pass through it into the birth canal. It is the most painful part of the whole labor process! Often, even when the mother has anesthesia going and has been relatively comfortable during the earlier stages of labor, she begins to feel pain and pressure. It signals, for the mother-to-be, the time to reposition her body for the birth. If she refuses to cooperate, it can lead to surgical intervention or even the death of the infant!

For the infant, the transition from womb to birth has to be very traumatic! All the baby knows is its nice, warm, cozy, liquid environment. It hears its mother's voice and feels her heart beat. All is secure in its little world. Then begins labor! At first, there is some pressure, some squeezing—not too bad so far. As time goes on, things go from bad to worse! It loses its water bath, the pressure increases, and becomes so frequent that it is hard for the baby to catch its breath. Then, when it seems like things can't possibly get any worse, transition happens! The baby is forced into a very tight place—so tight that the bones in its little skull have to overlap each other for it to fit! The squeezing goes on and on and on. It becomes almost impossible to get any oxygen. Then the top of the baby's head suddenly gets cold. *Cold*! What on earth is cold?!? All of a sudden, something grabs the baby's head, pulls it down while turning it, and boom! *Everything* is cold and bright and noisy! All of a sudden something very rough is being rubbed all over its body. That's it! Baby can't take anymore and begins to scream!

This is transition. According to Webster's, transition is defined as "Passage from one place or state to another; change; an event that results in a transformation."[19] In the birthing process, all of these things are happening. The parents understand that even though it is a painful, difficult, and tiring process it is absolutely necessary for both the mother and child to survive. They understand that for the baby to stay in the womb means certain death. They welcome their newborn into a broad, new, wonderful place that the baby could not have begun to imagine! What seemed like a very bad situation suddenly turns into a wonderful situation. All the baby is probably thinking is "Put me back!" It can't understand that its parents know what is best for it even though sometimes it is a painful process.

We are often like the baby. God really does know what is best for us. Sometimes, we've been in a particular environment for so long that it is no longer healthy for us to remain. Our Lord knows that there is a broad, new, wonderful place waiting for us and longs to birth it in us, but He also knows it is a painful process. He knows we may try to resist. He also knows who will allow Him to birth the new into them and who will resist. He knows who will reposition themselves for the birthing He wants to bring forth in their lives and who will refuse allowing that which He wants to birth in us die. We have to remember that we don't see what God sees. Do we trust Him enough to allow that which we have clung to for so long, that which has become old and stale in our lives to die? Do we trust Him enough to reposition ourselves for the birth even though we don't have a clue what it will look like?

I believed that I fully trusted God in everything. I believed that I could hear clearly from God and that He would tell me if there was a shift or change that I needed to make. Everything that I believed would be put to the test in the infamous year of 2011.

I mentioned that the year actually began for me in 2010. The ninth of Av is a very interesting date on the Jewish calendar. Both Jewish temples were destroyed on the ninth of Av. The Romans crushed the Bar Kokhba revolt killing over one hundred thousand Jews in 132 CE on this infamous day. The first crusade was declared by the Catholic pope in 1095 on the ninth of Av. It resulted in the death of ten thousand Jews in the first month alone! The Jews were expelled from England in 1290 and again from Spain in 1492 on the ninth of Av. World War I started in 1914 on this date that set the stage for the holocaust; and on this date in 1942, the mass deportation of Jews from the Warsaw ghetto to the death camps began.[20]

It all started when the ten spies came back from the Promised Land with the evil report about the giants. They declared that they could not defeat these giants even after all the miracles God had done for them (Numbers 13–14)! According to Jewish tradition, this occurred on the ninth of Av. They refused to reposition themselves for His birthing them into a broad, new place, and they died in the wilderness.

There is a twenty-one-day period leading up to the ninth of Av known as the time of "The Dire Straits." This was historically when the walls of Jerusalem were breached leading to the first temple destruction by Nebuchadnezzar in 586 BC. It is a time to put a guard over our minds and stand against the evil report that the enemy would like to dump on us. It is a time to reposition ourselves for what God wants to birth in us. It is a time to *repent* as necessary so we don't come into agreement with the enemy instead of with what God wants to do in our lives.

In 2010 during the season of the Dire Straits, I was distracted with caring for grandchildren, unable to spend the time with the Lord that I was accustomed to, and unaware of my own need for repentance. It set the stage for everything that was to come.

One of the first warnings I had that year was a prophecy brought forth by Chuck Pierce:

> There is death in the pot! I have brought you to the beginning of the river to break the death out of the waters that will flow in days ahead. There is a new river that is rising! For you have had one refreshing move and felt the river flowing in one way, but debris has gotten into My waters and blocked the way for your future. But like a stick of dynamite, I am coming in to re-empower you, and I am blowing open that blockade that has been blocked up. A new river movement now begins. I say to that demon of *Blockade*, "You now must let go and go! Blockade, let go, and GO!" For this river will be one that comes from a new spring. Don't try to go back to the spring that brought in the last river. Know that I am going deeper to bring forth a new spring in this place. Don't try to move in what flowed in one season, for you have seen nothing like the water that I am going to rise in your midst.[21]

I read it, but I didn't understand it.

The first "bad report" hit in December of 2010. (It was already 5771 on the Hebrew calendar.) A close relative had brought his girlfriend home, leaving his wife and three children reeling in the aftermath of adultery and betrayal. He was supposed to be a Christian. Jesus was supposed to be his Lord and Savior. We went and rescued his wife and children. There was no reasoning with him. He didn't love his wife and wanted a new start. I interceded, but the only thing I really felt a release for when I prayed was that everyone involved in this situation would be saved. One person has already met Jesus as of this writing, but I still anticipate many more salvations. The devil *cannot* win!

When I started the annual January twenty-one-day fast, the Lord spoke something very interesting to me. He said:

> 2011 will be a pivotal year similar to 1988, but up a notch. It will start with intense warfare and end with great breakthrough and victory. Remember it takes four years of growth and pruning for an olive tree to become productive. The olives go through a crushing and three pressings before all the oil is released.

I will never forget 1988. That was the year that started out with cancer and poverty but ended up with health, my first missions trip to Jamaica, and the meeting of my husband! Talk about a pivotal year! My whole life turned around that year! It was also a very painful year. Was 2011 going to be even more painful? Would I be crushed and pressed? I had been at this current duty station for four years. I was looking forward to the breakthrough and victory, the new oil, but I didn't know if I could weather the storm.

I also didn't know if I was really hearing from God or not. I seemed to be battling a lot of confusion. I wasn't sure if the dreams I was having, the words I was hearing, or the things I was sensing were actually from the Lord or from an overactive imagination. In the last year or two, my husband and I had drifted apart. He did his own thing and I did mine. I didn't share anything spiritual with him. I really didn't think he was interested. I did believe that he still loved me even if we didn't share the same spiritual goals. I shared a lot of what I was seeing and hearing with my pastor. It was my hope that the pastor would take these things to the Lord in prayer and help me sort it all out. I gave him permission to let me know if I was off base or not. I desperately wanted to make sure I was hearing right and that I was spiritually covered.

In March I had a dream. It was a very simple dream where my husband and I both had on shirts that buttoned down the front, and we were each missing some buttons on our shirts, but we had extra buttons sewn on the inside of our shirts that we could use to replace the missing buttons. Later that very day, as I was sharing this dream with my husband and what it could possibly mean, he just came right out and said that he didn't love me anymore and was thinking about getting a divorce!

I was floored! What is *this* attack all about!? At first I was in shock, unable to believe what I was hearing. This could not be happening to us. God sovereignly and supernaturally put us together. This just wasn't right! I begged him to go to counseling with me. I knew we had what we needed to fix the breach in our relationship. The pastor said he wasn't a marriage counselor but agreed to one session. That session didn't seem to do any good. Also, we were not the only couple in our church having marital problems. Other couples seemed on the verge of divorce. I knew it was spiritual. Somehow a covenant-breaking spirit had been allowed to come in and was wreaking havoc in the church!

Now I was fighting on three fronts. I was warring for my church, warring for my family, and warring for my own marriage. I felt overwhelmed but was somehow still confident of ultimate victory. The Lord did say that the year would end in breakthrough and great victory, so I clung to the promise.

Things got bad at church. My husband wouldn't sit with me. My family didn't know what to think. I continued to fast and pray, war and contend. I simply didn't know what else to do. My husband suggested we separate for a little while to see how he would feel about me when I wasn't home. I felt like this was not a good solution, that it was giving place to the enemy, but after a while I agreed and went to stay with a girlfriend for a couple of weeks.

It was refreshing being around my intercessor girlfriends. They listened to me, prayed for me, and were there for me. They prophesied the promises of God over me. They supplied me with a lifeline that I desperately needed. Now I had all these awesome promises from the Living God, but my circumstances looked dismal at best. I chose to stand on the promises. That's all I had.

In early May during my prayer time the Lord gave me this new word:

> One thing really lacking is death to your
> reputation. You don't always tell people what I
> want to say or when I want to say it for fear
> of offending them or hurting their feelings.
> You want people to like you and care too much
> what others think about you. I am allowing
> misunderstanding to build in the lives of those
> closest to you. The men you most trust will
> criticize you, judge you, and condemn you. You
> will die to the desire to defend yourself. I will
> vindicate you when the time is complete.

That's just great! Just what I needed to hear. As if things weren't bad enough, they were going to get worse, and I wasn't even going to be allowed to defend myself!

The Lord gave me several dreams that year about showers. I knew that indicated a need for cleansing, but for whom and from what? In the latest dream I found myself in a room with multiple showers. I was running water in a sink to get it warm. When it was warm, I turned the water off and turned to enter one of the showers, but another beat me to it. Then I went into another stall, but it was piled with clothes as was the third stall. The forth stall had clothes hanging from a line. I turned to my friend and said, "Let's get out of here and come back later." In the dream I understood that I had labored to get things ready for myself and others. Some are cluttering with clothing the area of their cleansing. We can't be clothed in the new until we are cleansed from the old. We have to get naked before God to be cleansed. I can't allow others to move me out of that which I have labored to attain. I need to be bold enough to remove all the old clutter from the stalls so we can all be cleansed. Little did I know how exposed I was about to become. Coming back later for cleansing would not be an option. This was a now thing, but I didn't understand.

Then I had another dream. In this dream I found myself wounded and bleeding in several places. I was following my husband trying to keep up with him. He was ignoring me. He went down into a wooded area to a cave that other men were also entering. I saw two other women there who, as they tried to enter the cave with their men, were shot several times and also left wounded and bleeding. Finally realizing that my husband didn't care about my condition, I asked someone to take me to a hospital where I could be healed. It was another warning dream, but I didn't have a clue what to do about it. I wrote in my journal that day: "The men are leaving us behind wounded and bleeding. They don't understand that we can't make it without each other."

Shortly after this last dream, one of my intercessor friends brought forth a prophecy that I knew was for me:

> I see you standing at the banks of the Red Sea with the Egyptian army at your back. You are asking God, "What do I do? I don't know what to do. Do I turn and fight? Run away?" The Lord says to stand still and see the salvation of the Lord. The children of Israel considered their options as well. It never occurred to them that I actually could or would part the sea, have

them cross over on dry ground, and drown all
their enemies. No precedent had yet been set
for this type of miracle. I am about to do a new
thing that you can't imagine. Stand still and let
me be God.

Well, at this point, that's all I could do. I was battle-
weary. I thought to myself, *At least I have a pastor who
will fight for me and pick me up when I am down. At least
I have some intercessor girlfriends who will stand with me.*
I didn't realize that things were about to get even worse
than they already were.

I'll never forget the "meeting" with the pastor in his
office. I should have known something was up when
one of his deacons was already there. My husband and
I went in and sat down. I was not overly concerned
because we had been friends with this pastor for many
years. He was very much in favor of things prophetic
and told me to make sure I told him whatever the Lord
showed me. I felt respected and approved by him. I felt
that I could tell him most anything; we were friends.
He and my husband rode motorcycles together and
spent time with each other. Nothing prepared me for
the bomb he was about to drop on me.

First, he counseled another in the meeting about
not sitting in the front row with her children; they were
too much of a distraction during the teaching. Then he
spoke with me and my husband. I don't recall exactly
what he said to my husband, but nothing could have
prepared me for what he said next. His countenance
was that of a stern authority figure, not a friend. He
told us that we were either going to have an amiable

divorce or an ugly one; it was our choice. He said nothing about us reconciling. He told me to step down from ministry until my husband and I got divorced. After that, we could talk about ministry again. He told me to hand over my key to the church, quit praying for the church and anyone and everyone including himself in his church! When I asked why, all he said was that people were talking.

I couldn't breathe. I was in shock. People are talking!?! Why are they talking and not helping my husband and I get through this thing? Why is this pastor giving place to all this gossip anyway? I poured out five years of my life in fasting and prayer and now that I'm under attack, all they can do is talk? On top of everything, I'm supposed to quit praying! I left his office, walked out of the church, got in my car, and went home. I was in tears. I've never cried so much in all my life. I could count on my fingers the number of times I'd cried in my whole life. I'm not a crier, but I couldn't take any more. I cried for three days. I couldn't stop. I didn't care if I lived or died. I had now lost everything: my husband, my family, my ministry, and my church family.

Through my tears, I asked the Lord, what went wrong? What did I miss? How did I screw up this time? In my journal I wrote:

> I'm in the place of devastation. I've been left for dead by the side of the road, wounded, broken and bleeding; kicked when I was down. Where is the grace and mercy I've heard preached so often? I've been misunderstood, judged, and condemned without a trial. I can't ever

see myself trusting this pastor again or even going back to his church. How could this have happened? How could I have misread this friendship, trusted this pastor with so much? Then the Lord spoke to me: *"You are out of alignment. When your back is out of alignment and you pick up something heavy, it throws your back out and you are laid up. You are out of spiritual alignment with your husband. When you picked up something spiritually heavy (the Masonic prayer event), it caused you to be laid out. Re-align with your husband."*

I repented.

Something so simple yet so profound. I fully believed I was covered by both my husband and my pastor when in reality I had no covering at all. I removed myself out from under my husband when I decided I could do all this spiritual warfare without him. I thought I was protecting him from all the attack when in reality I left him wide open to spirits of deception and confusion. Then, unknown to me, my pastor removed himself from covering me when he began to believe the lies of the enemy concerning me.

At the end of the three days, my husband and I began to really talk for the first time in a long time. He said that the pastor was convinced I was operating in a Jezebel spirit and had him convinced of it too! He said the pastor was actually encouraging him to divorce me! My husband said at first he thought the tears were part of an act I was playing, but then he realized it was real and something broke. He said he loved me and would be there for me! We began to rebuild our life together.

I always knew that I struggled to trust other people but felt that I could forgive others okay. I've had to forgive a lot of non-Christians for stuff, but I figured that the devil made them do it! Now, I was struggling to forgive. I couldn't understand how people who were supposed to love the Lord and love each other could so easily judge and condemn a brother or sister in Christ. I knew from the prophecy over a month earlier that I was not allowed to vindicate myself, but it turned out to not be a problem. No one seemed to care that I wasn't in church any longer.

I did word studies on trust and forgiveness. I had to make sense of what had happened. I wanted to understand where I was and how to proceed. I needed to be able to forgive unconditionally according to God's Word so I would be free. John 20:23 says that if I hold on to another's sins and don't forgive they are literally seized by strength. I didn't want to do that. What I really wanted was the memory of this pastor and what had happened to be completely gone from my mind!

The word *forgive* in the Hebrew is "Nasah," and it means to lift absolutely, accept, bear up, carry away, honor, and respect. I would eventually get to the place where I felt I could lift and carry away, but honor and respect? *That* would take some doing! Mark 6:14–15 commands us to forgive others their offenses, so I would have to work on it. The word translated into offenses literally means "side slips or unintentional error." I would have to be able to completely forgive. It was not going to be easy. I felt betrayed and left for dead. It was definitely not going to be easy!

In the course of my study of God's word about what had happened, I stumbled on a very interesting passage of scripture in James chapter 1. The chapter talks about persevering through trials, but this is the first time I had noticed verse 12: "Blessed is a man who perseveres under trial; for once he has been approved, he will receive the crown of life which the Lord has promised to those who love Him" (NASB). I remembered having asked the Lord for crowns sometime in the past. I guess I was working on the crown of life, but I had no idea it would be so hard!

My husband still attended that church. I went to church with my girlfriends. My husband tried to arrange a meeting with the pastor to talk things out, try to come to a reconciliation, but the pastor wouldn't do it. That pastor never spoke to me again. After a while, my husband felt estranged from the congregation as well, and he ceased attending. We began to attend another church where the messages really spoke to our hearts in the place where we were. We were beginning to heal.

My husband and I worked on our relationship. At that time, the Lord put a book in our hands that had been written years before but was exactly what we needed for that season.[22] We began to learn about our love languages. We realized that the things we did to express love to each other was really what we ourselves needed and that the reason our "love tanks" had been empty for so long was that we spoke different love languages!

We started discussing what we were going to do next. We had labored in several churches over the years and left each one on good terms. This was the first time anything like this had ever happened, and we were supposed to be good friends! At one point I had a dream that I was standing at the door to the church, but instead of the regular door with glass in it, there was a solid steel door in its place. It was obvious to me that the church was closed to us, and we would not be welcome there any longer. I had lost a church, but I had regained my husband! We were back in correct alignment with each other and really enjoying being together again.

I want to reiterate here that the real enemy in this was and will always be demonic forces. For a season, we were all trapped by the lies of the enemy, enveloped in darkness and deception. The level of warfare we found ourselves in was beyond anything any of us had ever encountered before. We didn't know how to process it. The Lord graciously pulled me and my husband out of it.

The Lord reminded me of the dream about the hippo (discussed in chapter 9) that lived in the pool behind the house and had muddied the waters. The church people were feeding it. I discovered that hippos often signify the principality known as the Behemoth spirit. The Lord showed me in prayer that Behemoth is large, impervious to woundings, is arrogant believing that nothing can phase it or stop it. It feeds on pride! Anytime there is a group of people who feel as though they are on the cutting edge of what God is doing and the other churches in the area are missing it, and perhaps not necessary to the Lord's kingdom purposes, it is my opinion that they are operating in pride. On an individual level, when we are convinced that we have the whole picture and we believe we are right and another is wrong, we've already judged and condemned that person. That is pride. We never have enough information to judge another person, especially their motivations.

It is also my opinion that this previous pastor did not intend evil; he was just deceived. He is not the enemy; the demons involved in this situation were the enemy. We were all under attack; we all made mistakes. We've not spoken since the attack took place, but I forgive him, bless him, and wish him well.

Shortly after the enemy successfully drove the dividing wedge, the Lord brought forth several prophecies that spoke to our situation and gave us some comfort. One of these was from Chuck Pierce:

> You will have a new place to stand. However, do not rush to establish your footing. In this new place, many changes will take place, so be willing to root and then be re-rooted. I am beginning to light your spirit within you in a new way. The sevenfold spirit within you is now being rekindled and brought to life so that we will become one with My Lamp Stand. You and I will become one in covenant alignment this season. We will begin to burn brightly as we move forward. The world will see the sevenfold Spirit that I have in the earth. This Spirit is beginning to burn again. Hell will not be able

to put that fire out. Many who are standing now will come alive and burn again. Though you stopped and stalled in the last season, you will advance in a way this season that you have not advanced before. I have one that builds and one that establishes. Then I have one that watches and keeps. Let me help you find your place this hour. Let me help you get established, for I am transplanting many from one garden to another garden. I am causing some seed to grow that did not grow last season. I am plowing new furrows, breaking old soil, but creating new fields. I will grow a troop for this season. This is the troop that begins to move and advance in a new way.[23]

This prophecy confirmed what my husband and I were sensing that God was moving us into a whole new thing, a whole new place that we couldn't imagine! I so needed a change in atmosphere! We needed healing from all the battle wounds we had sustained in the last season. We just had to be careful not to make any assumptions. The Lord spoke to us not to make any long-term plans, so we decided to go visit grandchildren and then head south for the winter. We would wait on God for what He had for us next.

It's amazing what a change in atmosphere can do! I felt lighter, happier than I had been in a long time. I was no longer under the weight of that oppressive atmosphere from the last season. I began to hear more clearly from the Lord than I had in a long time. I had been feeling that my identity, my calling, was over. I was no longer praying prophetically. It wasn't in me anymore. I didn't know what to do. I had been involved in intercessory prayer ministries for so long that I could not see myself doing anything else. I went to an intercessor's conference and an interesting thing happened. Even before the worship began on the first night, the apostolic leader stood up and prophesied that someone had been told to "sit down and shut up," and if that person would come forward, the curse would be broken off of her. That was me! She prayed over me, and I felt a heavy weight lift. The curse was broken! God was not finished with me yet!

A couple of months later, this prophecy came forth, again from Chuck Pierce:

> *There have been many things at the bottom of the pile that I am bringing to the top of the pile.* There have been many things that have been hidden that I am bringing up. You have even kept things hidden because you've not expressed Me in the way that I am calling you to express Me this season. *Express Me now and what is hidden will come to the top.* Your position that has been secluded will come out into the open. Praise Me now and watch things rise to the surface.
>
> I'm going deeper because you've been plucked up wrong. There are miracles deep within you that I am ready to reveal to you. I'm going to unplug some things and re-plug other things. *This will be a time of unplugging, checking your circuits, and re-plugging.* So watch Me redo your circuit board for I am a God of power. Once I re-plug some things within you and I reorder and rewire some things,

your eyes will see in a way you could not see. Do not yield to the accusation of the enemy in this hour. There has been an accusation hurled at My people called "Mistaken Identity." Many feel accused they are someone that they are not. Many have been trapped in a maze of 'Mistaken Identity.' Running from the accuser in a labyrinth of fear and confusion, some have been captured and have compromised. Pray! The enemy seeks to pull many back into traumas of the past through the threat of accusation. Buckle not under the threat, but hide under the shadow of My Wing—for this is a season of covering. I cover you and will deliver you. Do not yield to 'Mistaken Identity!' Stand in *Your Identity*. Set your face like flint and stand in your identity in Christ. You will stand in the shaking, you will come forth in the plans of God, and you will know your identity in this season.[24]

The year of transition was finally over. We were being birthed into a broad, new place that we could not even begin to imagine, and God was the one in charge of the birthing!

The Promises

The enemy lives to steal our dreams, cram us into a pit of hopelessness and mediocrity, and destroy our destiny. Jesus came to give us abundant life. We are created in His image with the ability to dream, to imagine, and to create. The enemy almost succeeded in stealing the dream and my destiny—but God!

It took me a long time to recover from the year of devastation and the disappointment and the betrayal that went with it. Some of you are probably thinking, "I don't get what she's talking about. After all, she didn't end up divorced, destitute, and on the streets. No one in her immediate family died." All that's true, but you have to understand that I poured my life, everything I was, into seeing true revival break out along route 66. It was God's dream for my whole life, the purpose for which I was created, my part in His kingdom plan! I felt like a failure, and I'm not getting any younger. I probably don't have another twenty years to start over again.

Many never recover from their devastations. They stay trapped in the trauma of the past, losing the dream, never fulfilling their destiny. It is my opinion that we all end up in some kind of prison at one time or another.

Sometimes it is a prison of our own making. Sometimes we are falsely accused and imprisoned. Often we don't know exactly how we got there, but we do know that we really don't want to take any more chances in life that might put us back.

Dutch Sheets had an interesting comment about losing our dream in prison. He spoke of a man in prison, who after he got out, made a very successful life for himself. When this man was asked how he managed this, he replied, "Unlike the other prisoners, I never decorated my cell."[25] Dutch proceeded to say: "Decorating one's cell means we have resolved ourselves to making a current rut permanent. Cells come in all shapes and sizes. If allowed, they will imprison you in a confined place of isolation, despair, hopelessness, and inactivity. Their ultimate effect, if not checked, will be to rob you of your future."[26]

I've already had too many times in my life when I "decorated my cell" by making ultimatums about risks I would never take to protect myself because of the trauma of the past. Realistically, only God is really able to protect us. It reminds me of the many times I would be driving down the road and see a turtle attempting to cross it. Often the turtle would see the oncoming traffic, but instead of racing across the road away from danger, it would retreat into its shell only to be squashed anyway! Sometimes in the attempt to protect ourselves from the traffic of life, we instead seal the death of our dream and our destiny.

Dutch Sheets went on to say: "A while back I went through a season of hope deferred that tried to force me to stop dreaming. Simultaneously, I experienced significant betrayal and broken promises. While in this season, I realized that in some areas of my life, I had subconsciously began to shut down. As the results intensified, the inevitable decrease in creativity began. Only dreamers create. Non-dreamers sustain and eventually stagnate."[27] I really identified with what Dutch was saying, and I knew what had happened, but I didn't know that I had begun to shut down also. I felt stagnant and adrift but didn't know how to regain my mooring.

I did, however, have promises. The Lord told me not to lose my identity in Him. He let me know that this surgery, even though painful, was necessary. After all, a surgeon will not waste hours of his time on someone who will be dead shortly anyway! God expected me to live and step into the promises He had for me! "Since God never acts without purpose, the fact that you're alive is proof that you have something this generation needs."[28]

In the midst of the storm of the last season, I attended a women's conference and received an unusual prophecy from someone I had never met and who knew nothing about me. She said from the Lord:

> You are a standard-bearer; one who holds up the flags in battle to see which way the winds are blowing. The standard-bearer had to be there to keep the armies moving. I see you as one who has that standard high and lifted up. You don't want there to be compromise. You don't want there to be sin. You don't want the ranks to fall

apart. You just have a heart that says, "Oh come on, this has got to work; we've got to have truth; we've got to have holiness." You are set in the body of Christ to bear the standard, and the Word of the Lord comes to you: "Don't let it down, don't let it down." Although others round about you say, "You're holding it too high, you're being too stubborn." You don't yield, you don't give up. "Hold it up," says the Lord, for without the standard-bearer the army would surely fail, the battle would surely be lost. So I call you to be a woman of courage. I call you to be a woman of fortitude and conviction. I call you to be a forerunner says the Lord to lead forth the charge by holding up the standard.

Another prophecy I received at that conference further comforted and encouraged me:

Daughter, you have taken Me by the hand and allowed Me to lead you, and your obedience has opened doors and the doors I have opened for you, no man can close. There are more open doors ahead of you. The sum of your deeds is written in the books and there are things written that you will be walking in that you don't even know yet. There's a whole volume written that you're going to be walking in. You haven't seen anything yet. All that you have done is nothing compared to what's going to be done. The Lord said that there is multiplication upon you. There's an ability upon you to train, equip, and release. You want everyone He sends to you to be equipped, stable, and able to stand on their own two feet and reproduce. You are a reproducer of reproducers. You have an anointing to teach others about the Holy Spirit and how to function in the gifts of the Spirit. There are things that the Lord has placed on the inside of you that is natural to you, as normal as breathing to you. I see you with jewels in your hand. You've pulled out a treasure box with jewels of revelation. He's going to teach you what they mean. I see a ruby, a diamond, a sapphire, and an emerald. These are jewels from the Presence of God. The Lord said you are one of His diamonds—there's a brilliancy about you. There is a purity and depth in you. He is proud of you. You are going to go far, wide and deep. There's a real ability in you to manifest the love of God.

At that point all I could see was the "diamond" part. After all, diamonds are forged under tremendous pressure, and I had really felt pressed and pressured! I clung to the promises. I read and reread them. They were my lifeline back from the brink of despair.

My husband never really liked where we were living. Now we had no reason to stay; nothing to hold us there. We needed a place to heal. We knew about the Brownsville Revival in Pensacola, Florida, and we also knew that John Kilpatrick had started another church in Mobile, Alabama that was experiencing revival, so we decided to head for the Alabama Gulf Coast. What awaited us there was beyond anything we could imagine!

In October right after the year of transition was over, Chuck Pierce brought forth another interesting prophecy. At first, I wasn't sure it applied to us, but after further reflection, it fit like a glove:

> Many of your pots have turned over from the past. Many things have spilled out onto the ground, things that you thought were detrimental to any future that you had. But even what was hard that has spilled out into the earth I can now cause to blossom. I can strip open, open up and I can fling wide what needs to be flung wide on your behalf. *This is now a new season for what has been poured out to come back in a different way.* Gather your pots! Gather your pots! Gather your pots, for I am going to fill them beyond what you thought they could be filled!
>
> I am moving you into a season. I am going to surprise you. I am going to reconcile you with your heart's desire. I am going to restore you. I am going to unlock you. I am going to cause things that have been held up from you, to be released to you. I am going to declare what was a trauma to become a blessing. I am going to cause you to walk into blessings you never thought you would walk into.[29]

We had no idea what was awaiting us. At first, we attended Sunday services. The presence of God was deeper and richer than anywhere we'd ever attended before. The worship took us into the Holy of Holies. That, however, was not all! It seemed like almost every message that was brought forth whether it was through John Kilpatrick, his son John Michael, or Nathan Morris was tailor-made for us for healing. Every week God was pouring oil on our wounds, breathing new life into our damaged souls, giving us a future and a hope (Jeremiah 29:11).

One Sunday morning John Kilpatrick read a prophecy that astounded us:

> I declare by the Spirit of God that a seven year season, a now season of jubilee, is upon the church. It is a time to rejoice because God is indeed making your enemies His footstool. Literally right now, as you hear this, God is at work vindicating you. He's busy behind the scenes working on your behalf. A new seven year period of great spiritual release is upon you. The years of persecution & suffering for His Name's sake are about to pay off big time. The year that we have just ended has marked the end of a brutal season for many of you. At first we did not discern the magnitude of what we have come through, but now there is a supernatural season that we are experiencing, and I believe that it is an awesome church-wide, go to the next level, unprecedented, supernatural shift. One supernatural season has ended and a distinctly new and better supernatural season in God has begun. Unnoticed by most, the Holy Spirit began to move about mid-January, setting off a chain reaction of spiritual events for all who have endured hardship as a solder of Jesus. If you've been enduring hardship, if

you've been wounded, especially by friendly fire, this new season is just for you. God said he's going to heal you. In a word, this new season is all about vindication. It's not about you exacting vengeance. It's not about you getting even. Instead it's about vindication from God. For the past seven years as you have endured suffering as His faithful solder, God said you're about to be rewarded. The truth is about to come out. You're about to be freed from alleged charges against you. You're about to be absolved and acquitted, and the Lord is about to pronounce over you "not guilty." Victims are about to rejoice and accusers are about to be silenced. The Lord said you're not being paroled, you're being acquitted. I believe that many believers just like you have lived through a seven year period of great personal hardship, especially in the area of damaged or even severed personal or ministry relationships. The Lord said all this is going to change and it's going to change rapidly. If you've been victimized by sinners or saints, get ready, your day is right at hand. Specifically you've been waiting for vindication from past injustices, betrayal and abandonments and the subsequent disillusionment it has created. Frankly, the root problem has been about witchcraft in the church. A spirit of witchcraft that has decimated and dissected you is finally being exposed. You paid a great price for your integrity, your character, and your honesty. It cost you a great deal to be a true follower of Jesus Christ. You may have appeared to many to be a bad guy when in fact, you are actually the victim of a spiritual crime. Again, all that's going to change. The Lord would say to you today, your days of mourning are over, and your jubilee has now just begun. I declare over you that a season of vindication and long overdue justice, especially if you are one of His leaders, is upon you. God has already begun the necessary process of vindicating you. You've suffered betrayal, false accusation, broken promises and abandonment long enough, God said. As a result, you've been disillusioned about the call on your life far too long. The Lord said, "Be encouraged." He's delivering you from the results of past problems, the results of past situations, and circumstances that has either delayed or in some extreme cases has actually robbed you of your destiny. God said, "I say to you, all will be as it's supposed to be." There will be no part of your destiny delayed any longer and no part of your destiny will be denied. Is there anything too hard for Me? Indeed, this vindication is a key word. It's a now word from the Lord and I hear it in my spirit loud and clear for you. To all of His wonderful and wounded warriors, to all who have been suffering abuse at the hands of others, the Lord would comfort you with these words in this season. I am vindicating you. You are being exonerated. You are about to experience true justice. You are now about to experience the promotion in God that you waited patiently for. The seven years of explosive increase, of power, gifting, and authority is now yours for the taking. You are going to the next level for sure. The promises of

God in your life are now about to be wonderfully fulfilled very quickly. Here's the part you need ears to hear: whether this prophecy affects you will depend on your proper response. No doubt, you will be asked by God to participate in this healing and restoration process of formerly broken relationships especially with Christians. Please do so graciously and humbly, just as Christ would. Say "yes" to any and all who are looking to be reconciled with you. I predict that people saved and unsaved from your past will soon be calling and visiting you. They will come with olive branches in their hands looking to establish peace with you. I urge you to accept their offering and participate enthusiastically in the peace process. God's part in this seven year season will be to vindicate you. Like Joseph coming out of your dungeon, you are about to experience great favor on your life. A true season of amazing promotion is awaiting you. So welcome to your new seven year season of jubilee!

Wow! The Lord has heard my cry from His Holy hill! If ever a prophecy was for anyone, this one was for me. Thank you, Jesus! God said I would be healed. He promised the next level of power, gifting and authority and all I have to do is wait on Him, trust and believe. I don't have to start all over again. He really did keep that which I committed to Him for this day.

Last spring, the Lord gave me another dream. In this dream I was running through some gates calling after a Mr. Duncan. It was my understanding that he was contemplating suicide. After I awoke, I went into prayer, but didn't sense that the dream was literal. The Lord said there was a deeper meaning, and He told me to look up the name "Duncan." When I did, what I found was very interesting. Duncan is Celtic in origin and it means Fortress Warrior. The motto on the coat of arms means "Learn to endure"![30]

I think that the interpretation of this dream is obvious. I'm still His warrior. He called me specifically to be a fortress warrior, to labor for the pulling down of strongholds or fortresses (2 Corinthians 10:4–5). These strongholds are prideful speculations contrary to the will of God. I'm a standard-bearer. I have to hold the standard of holiness high. "Mature believers," especially ministers, aren't too happy with this message when it is directed to them personally, but it is necessary. I asked the Lord a long time ago why revival was so delayed. He asked me how many Ananias and Sapphiras am I willing to bury. I told Him none, so I have to labor and wait for the promise. I have to learn to endure hardship as a good soldier of Jesus (2 Timothy 2:3). I can't allow my calling, my destiny to die.

It took twenty-six years to realize who I really am, what I was called to do, and who to be. I was reminded of the dream once again of the king with the scepter and the crown. We went together into the house not for the purpose of bringing in revival, but for the purpose of cleansing His house. I was His fortress warrior. I was called to tear down fortresses and bring in holiness, but all these years I *thought* I was praying in revival! Over and over sin was exposed, but revival never came. Disappointment came on the heels of unmet expectations. But God.

The Alabama gulf coast is a place of white, sandy beaches, and mild climate. The sun shines here most of the time. The restaurants cook up some of the most awesome seafood in lively, colorful settings overlooking watery vistas. We watch pelicans and herons fish. What a perfect place to heal and begin to dream again!

We were here for a couple of months when my husband decided he wanted a boat. All around us were beautiful waters teeming with fish of every variety. Having our own boat would mean access to deep sea fishing whenever we wanted to go instead of waiting for the occasional charter trip. He started shopping for fishing vessels and found what appeared to be a good boat for a great price!

I wasn't so sure about it. Buying a boat is expensive enough, but then we had to add maintenance and fuel to the cost. Did God really want us to own a fishing vessel? I prayed about it and didn't sense anything negative. I even felt like maybe God had a purpose for the boat; although, I couldn't imagine what that would be. Then Chuck Pierce brought forth another prophecy! One of these days I'm gonna have to talk to Chuck about all these strategically timed prophecies! He said in part:

> Praise Me seven days to be released from the anxiety and stress that have held you captive! Seven days of praise! *For I am shifting you and setting your boat upright* (emphasis my addition). I am going to heal how you got bruised in the

last season. I am going to remove reproaches off of you that have been hanging on to you. I'm going to do a new thing in you. Submit and go the right way. Don't lean on your own understanding. Walk with Me through and I will stand, protect you and justify the route I have asked you to take.[31]

We bought the boat.

No longer were we just "going south for the winter." The longer we stayed in Alabama, the more we liked it. Yea, I really missed my girlfriends, but now we lived in a vacation paradise where hopefully family and friends will come to visit!

Recently, when I was going back through my journals in preparation for the writing of this story, I came across an interesting dream from two years ago; well before the year of transition took place. In the dream my husband was packing up the RV. He said we were going someplace far away, but he wouldn't tell me. In the dream I suspected that we were going to the Gulf Coast! How's *that* for confirmation!

Well, here we are—living in paradise, fishing off our own boat out in the Gulf of Mexico, soaking and healing at Church of His Presence and the Bay of the Holy Spirit Revival. I still haven't connected locally with any of the believers or intercessors, but that will come in time. I don't intend to lose Mr. Duncan!

Conclusion

The loss of a loved one, a close friend, or a relative; the loss of a career with nowhere to turn; betrayals and abandonment; a debilitating injury or illness, physical or sexual abuse—these are all life-altering events. The enemy of our souls will make sure that all of us at one time or another goes through one or more of these events. Our lives are never the same afterward. Whether we transition into a new positive level or become trapped by the trauma of the past is up to us. We can cry out to Yeshua, Jesus, the lover of our souls to kiss the hurt, the wounds, and make them better.

Once again, it is the time of the year when the declarations we make, the confession of our mouths will sow the seed for our future for either good or evil. We can choose to stand on the promises the Lord has given us or continue to soak in our circumstances, declaring, "Oh woe is me."

This is not the end of this story. Oh no, it is but the beginning of a new chapter, a new season. What will it look like? I have no idea, but my heavenly Father has it all planned out!

"For I know the plans that I have for you,"
declares the LORD, "plans for welfare and not
for calamity to give you a future and a hope."

Jeremiah 29:11 (NASB)

I want to close with one last prophecy from Chuck
Pierce with Glory of Zion Ministries on Feb. 22, 2012:

I begin you one way, but I end you another way.
I begin you on a foundation and I cause your
covering to be placed in a new way. *Check your
foundation and then watch your covering form.* As
I rebuild your foundation, and as I align it with
the Head, with the covering that I am opening
over you, you will reach a place of critical
mass, a place of great momentum. Guard your
momentum and move with Me. The cover that
I am putting over you is woven together; it is
manifold, and it is filled with My wisdom. Ask
for this wisdom to penetrate you for this hour;
ask and you will be filled in a new way. There
will not be a thing that I cannot reveal to you.
Ask, ask, and watch wisdom come down. For
I am Jehovah Jireh, and I will come down and
show you provision that you've not seen. I am
Jehovah Jireh and I will come down and cover
you, and the provision you've been looking for,
I will reveal to you.

So come and sacrifice, and lay your vision
from last season before Me. Lay down that
which you have counted on, place it on My
altar, and watch Me come down and reveal new
provision and new sound, and reveal that which
was hidden in past seasons to you. *You will*

cause the top of that which you are standing on to be formed, and a covering to form over you. I will cover you with the shadow of My wing. I am putting together that which will mantle you in days ahead. Bring your vision and submit it, the vision of what you have been shown. Submit vision to Me, and watch provision come down in a new way. Even during this watch, you have been forming a portal that is now beginning to open above you, and the covering you've longed for is now coming down. You have felt many times that you were uncovered, and you have felt abandoned and felt like you were the only one standing. But because you have come during this watch, I will cover you in a new way.

I am covering you in a way that you will not be under the structure from the last seven years that you've been under. But you will be wearing a garment that will extend you into the next seven years.

The top is greater. The greater covering is coming over you today. You're being covered in a new way. You're clearing out. *Even that which you've learned in the last seven years will now begin to explode into new dimensions of wisdom, and new dimensions of insights.* You will teach others in simple ways. What you have gained knowledge of, you'll be able to multiply in teaching others. One word will not only fell the enemy, but one word will multiply in My people.

For just as with Peter, the foundation you were standing on would have caused you to sink down under. *But now I am lifting you up, and I am pulling you up, and I am taking you across into a new place.* And in this new place, there is an opening and an access for you that will multiply simple nuggets that are within you. They will expand, and they will begin to open up in new ways. And one thing you have gathered in the past season will now become a hundred in this season.

And even the way you've been standing, I'm changing your stance today. For you've been standing in one way, but now I'm causing you to rise up. And as I cover you, I will also come beneath you. I will be the wind that causes you to rise up above circumstances. I will be the rock that you stand on. I will not only be the cliff that you hide in, but I will cause you to soar in new ways.[32]

I'm claiming *this* promise too!

Appendix A

Bevere, John. *The Fear of the Lord*. Lake Mary, FL: Charisma House, 1997.

Bevere, John. *Under Cover*. Nashville, TN: Thomas Nelson, 2001.

Greenwood, Rebecca. *Authority to Tread*. Grand Rapids, MI: Chosen Books, 2005.

Heidler, Robert D. *The Messianic Church Arising!* Denton, TX: Glory of Zion, 2006.

Hill, Craig. *The Ancient Paths*. Littleton, CO: Family Foundations, 1992.

Jackson, John Paul. *Needless Casualties of War*. Fort Worth, TX: Streams, 1999.

Joyner, Rick. *The Vision*. Nashville, TN: Thomas Nelson, 2000.

Otis, George, Jr. *Informed Intercession*. Ventura, CA: Renew Books, 1999.

Pierce, Chuck D., and Rebecca Wagner Sytsema. *The Future War of the Church*. Ventura, CA: Regal Books, 2007.

Pierce, Chuck D. *Interpreting the Times*. Lake Mary, FL: Charisma House, 2008.

Pierce, Chuck D. *Redeeming the Time*. Lake Mary, FL: Charisma House, 2009.

Pierce, Chuck D. *Time to Defeat the Devil*. Lake Mary, FL: Charisma House, 2011.

Pierce, Chuck D., ed. *Reordering Your Day: Understanding and Embracing the Four Prayer Watches*. Denton, TX: Glory of Zion, 2006.

Pierce, Chuck D., and John Dickson. *The Worship Warrior*. Ventura, CA: Regal Books, 2002.

Sheets, Dutch. *Dream*. Minneapolis, MN: Bethany House, 2012.

Sheets, Dutch, and Chuck D. Pierce. *Releasing the Prophetic Destiny of a Nation*. Shippensburg, PA: Destiny Image, 2005.

Sheets, Dutch. *Intercessory Prayer*. Ventura, CA: Regal Books, 1996.

Sheets, Dutch. *Watchman Prayer*. Ventura, CA: Regal Books, 2000.

Stone, Perry. *40 Days of Teshuvah*. Cleveland, TN: Voice of Evangelism, 2006.

Stone, Perry. *Purging Your House, Pruning Your Family Tree*. Lake Mary, FL: Charisma House, 2011.

Wagner, Doris M., ed. *How to Minister Freedom*. Ventura, CA: Regal Books, 2005.

Notes

1   James Strong, S.T.D., LL.D., *Strong's Exhaustive Concordance*, [Electronic Version], from <http://www.e-sword.net>, 1890.

2   John. J. Parsons, *A Year Through the Torah: A Week-by-Week Journey for Christians,* (Scottsdale: Hebrew Heart Publications, 2008), 24.

3   Hal Lindsey, and Carole C. Carlson, *The Late, Great Planet Earth*, Grand Rapids: Zondervan, 1970.

4   Perry Stone, *Voice of Evangelism*, <http://www.voe.org/>.

5   Chuck Pierce, *Glory of Zion International Ministries*, <http://www.gloryofzion.org/>.

6   Curt Landry, *House of David Ministries*, <http://www.houseofdavid.us/>.

7   James Strong, S.T.D., LL.D., *Strong's Exhaustive Concordance*, [Electronic Version], from http://www.e-sword.net, 1890.

8   Joseph Stalin was the dictator of the Soviet Union from 1928 to 1953 and is reported to be responsible for over 30 million deaths of his own people.

9   Wikipedia, "Long Walk of the Navajo", Accessed June 11, 2012, <http://en.wikipedia.org/wiki/Long_Walk_of_the_Navajo>.

10 Chuck D. Pierce, ed., *Reordering Your Day: Understanding and Embracing the Four Prayer Watches*, Denton, TX: Glory of Zion, 2006.

11 Perry Stone, *40 Days of Teshuvah*, (Cleveland: Voice of Evangelism, 2006), 58.

12 Ibid., 59.

13 Ibid., 60–61, 67.

14 Chuck D. Pierce, *Interpreting the Times: Prophetic Insight and Strategic Oversight 2008*, DVD, Denton, TX: Glory of Zion, 2008.

15 "Famous Navy Quotes: Who Said Them and When." *Naval History and Heritage Command*, accessed June 25, 2012, <http://www.history.navy.mil/trivia/trivia02.htm>.

16 Chuck D. Pierce, *Glory of Zion Ministries*, "Your Piece is Important! Reach Down Deep Within You! There is Blessing that Needs to Unlock!" E-mail from the author, accessed Jan. 2010, <www.gloryofzion.org>.

17 The counting of the Omer is the 50 day period of time between Passover and Pentecost (Feast of Weeks). According to author Robert D. Heidler in his book "The Messianic Church Arising!" (Denton, TX: Glory of Zion, 2006), this is the time of a "massive outpouring of joyful giving and praise". "As we do this, it positions us to receive… the Fire of His Glory"! (pg 186).

18 William Sudduth, "Freemasonry 50 State Tour". R. a.m. Ministry, accessed July 2, 2012. <http://www.ramministry.org/news.htm>

19 "Definition: Transition." Webster's Online Dictionary with Multilingual Thesaurus Translation, accessed July 5, 2012, <http://www. websters-online-dictionary.org/definitions/ transition>.

20 Wikipedia. "Tisha B'Av." accessed July 5, 2012, < http://en.wikipedia.org/wiki/Tisha_B%27Av>.

21 Chuck D. Pierce, *Glory of Zion Ministries*. E-mail notice from the author, accessed January 27, 2010, <www.gloryofzion.org>.

22 Gary D Chapman, *The 5 Love Languages: The Secret to Love That Lasts*, Chicago: Northfield Publishing, 2010.

23 Chuck D. Pierce, *Glory of Zion Ministries*. E-mail notice from the author, accessed July 8, 2011, <www.gloryofzion.org>.

24 Chuck D. Pierce, *Glory of Zion Ministries*, E-mail notice from the author, accessed December 10, 2011, <www.gloryofzion.org>.

25 Dutch Sheets, *Dream: Discovering God's Purpose for your Life*, (Minneapolis. Bethany House, 2012), 57.

26 Ibid, 57.

27 Dutch Sheets, *Dream: Discovering God's Purpose for your Life*, (Minneapolis. Bethany House, 2012), 43.

28 Ibid, 50.

29 Chuck D Pierce, *Glory of Zion Ministries*. E-mail notice from the author, accessed October 15, 2011, <www.gloryofzion.org>.

30 "The Internet Surname Database", accessed April 30, 2012, < http://www.surnamedb.com/>.

31 Chuck D. Pierce, *Glory of Zion Ministries*, E-mail notice from the author, accessed February 1, 2012, <www.gloryofzion.org>.

32 Chuck D. Pierce, *Glory of Zion Ministries*, E-mail notice from the author, accessed February 22, 2012, <www.gloryofzion.org>.